Sailing ships

Sailing ships

Patrick Brophy

Hamlyn

London New York Sydney Toronto

Published by
The Hamlyn Publishing Group Limited
London · New York · Sydney · Toronto
Astronaut House, Feltham,
Middlesex, England

© Copyright
The Hamlyn Publishing
Group Limited 1974
ISBN 0 600 37977 9

Filmset in England by
V. Siviter Smith Limited, Birmingham

Printed in England by
Butler and Tanner Limited, Frome

Contents

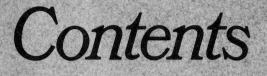

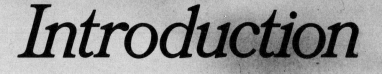

Introduction

The subject of this book is the whole history of sailing ships as a means of transport from the beginning of history to the present day. That is a very big subject for one rather small book and I have selected and compressed my material ruthlessly—and quite personally. I have omitted, either by design or ignorance, not only particular ships but whole classes of vessels: it is inevitable that my selection will not be yours and I apologise in advance for my omissions. Much of the early history of sail is speculation and where there is speculation there is argument—I have tried to present the arguments that seem to me to be most plausible but I make no claims to infallibility.

What I have tried to do in the following pages is to show, in broad outline, how ships have developed in response to the demands of trade and how that development has been channelled along the lines determined by the then-current state of technology and the availability of materials. This process has always been gradual—mainly because a ship represents a sizeable capital outlay and few investors are prepared to adventure their money on an expensive experiment.

All the chapters are necessarily brief so my hope must be to stimulate the appetite, not to satisfy it. The challenge of the sea was accepted by men who knew less of their destination than the astronauts knew of the moon, and the construction of their ships was an art rather than a science, but with courage, perseverance and ingenuity our forbears sought out every corner of the world. If this book encourages anyone to search for more information about the ships they sailed in and their methods of finding their way about the world, I shall be satisfied.

Chapter one

The birth of ships as transport

If you give a boy a lake and a log he will very rapidly invent the ship. When he has got as far as the raft he has invented the merchant ship–fit to carry cargoes of silks and pearls and ginger beer to the very edge of the world. The simple addition of a prevailing wind together with a coat or shirt, or even a leafy branch, and he has reinvented the sailing merchantman–the subject of this book. Sail-driven rafts are, in fact, capable of covering immense distances, as Thor Heyerdahl has shown in the *Kon Tiki* and the *Ra*.

The earliest records of sailing merchantmen come from Egypt. This is no accident: it is due to three interlocking factors–the people, the place, and the climate. The Egyptians already had a highly developed civilization five thousand years ago; the basis for the continuous prosperity on which a true culture must be founded is trade, and such a culture is bound to have developed some form of written language. The life of Egypt depended first and foremost on the River Nile. This great river not only ensured the fertility of the corn which was the wealth of the Empire but also provided the simplest means of heavy transport. The development of sailing ships in ancient Egypt was also helped by the local weather conditions–the prevailing winds blow in a southerly direction throughout the year whereas the Nile flows north. So, during the Age of the Pyramids, which began about 3000 BC, the stone-carrying ships of the Pharoahs had the advantage of a fair wind on the long hard voyage upstream to the quarries and then returned loaded, sails furled and mast lowered, carried by the Nile herself.

The original Egyptian ships were made of bundles of reeds lashed together. They were probably first in the form of a squarish raft, becoming, as experience accumulated, more pointed towards the ends and generally 'boat-shaped'. Later these served as a pattern for the building of wooden ships, a necessary development as greater size and strength was required. Due to the absence of timber of any size in Egypt the ships were not constructed of planks over a frame of ribs and keel, but made of short thick timbers pinned sideways to one another. The strength of this method of construction relies on the thickness of the 'shell' and the strength of the fastenings. Water pressure held the underwater body together while woven longitudinal lashings served the same purpose above the waterline.

By the middle of the third millenium BC the Egyptians had developed a fair sea-going trade in the Eastern Mediterranean, trading with both the Cretans and the Phoenicians. In 1500 BC Queen Hatshepsut sent a fleet of five sea-going ships to Punt, in East Africa, to trade for myrrh. These ships sailed from the Nile to the Red Sea through a channel which served the same purpose as the Suez Canal and on down the east coast of Africa. After reaching Punt–its location is now unknown but it may have been in the region of Ethiopia–the sailors traded successfully and returned safely to their queen. The story of this expedition can be seen carved on the walls of the temple at Deir-el-Bahari, near Thebes. One interesting feature of these later sea-going ships is the device the Egyptians employed to prevent them 'hogging', or drooping at the ends due to their length (which was in the region of eighty to ninety feet). This consisted of an enormous rope fastened to the ship at either end and supported along its length over a row of forked posts. This rope, as can be clearly seen in the contemporary carvings, was tensioned by twisting it like a tourniquet or, in sailors' slang, a 'Spanish windlass'. This problem of 'hogging' remained right up to the nineteenth century and explains why few wooden ships of much over two hundred feet long have ever been built. The *Victory,* for example, is 226 feet 3 inches long from figurehead to taffrail (the uppermost, aftermost part of her stern). As a measure of the Egyptian shipwrights' skill and the capacity of the ships they built, an inscription at Deir-el-Bahari refers to a barge for transporting 'the two obelisks at Elephantine'. One of these obelisks still stands in front of the temple of Amon Ra at Karnak. It is nearly a hundred feet high and weighs some three hundred and fifty tons. This means that a barge capable of carrying the pair must have been about two hundred feet long and seventy to eighty feet wide with a laden displacement of some one thousand five hundred tons–comparable to the ubiquitous coastal steamers of today.

The Phoenicians and Cretans, who took over the maritime supremacy of the Eastern Mediterranean as the Egyptian power declined, developed two quite distinct types of ship. One was a long, narrow, point-ended galley, propelled primarily by oars. This ship was designed for speed and, with its lack of cargo space, its need for an uneconomically large crew and

An Egyptian sailing ship, dating from the
Old Kingdom (2494–2345 BC). The ship is
running south under sail with the oarsmen
resting at their oars under the shade of an
awning. Many stays are needed to brace
the mast against the pull of the sail. Tomb
of Ti, Sakkara.

Opposite top: An Attic black-figure cup by Nikosthenes, *circa* sixth century BC. The vessels illustrated on this cup are more properly 'long ships' but they illustrate the twin steering oars and banana-shape of early Mediterranean shipping. Musée du Louvre, Paris.

Opposite bottom: A first-century BC Phoenician merchant ship. This relief on a sarcophagus from Sidon shows how closely Phoenician ships resembled contemporary Roman ships. They even copied the Roman artemon. National Museum, Beirut.

Below: The port of Ostia, first century AD. A variety of shipping–large and small merchantmen and rowing boats–appear in this busy relief. The stays of the merchantman on the left are set up with 'deadeyes', still in use in older boats today. Galleria Torlonia, Rome.

its aggressive 'ram', was a warship pure and simple. The other type was the 'round ship'. This was a near double-ended, broad, rather flat-bottomed sailing ship only rarely provided with oars. It was to be the basis of Mediterranean–and indeed European–merchantmen in the centuries to come. This distinction between the 'narrow ship' and the 'round ship' is not peculiar to the Mediterranean; it is to be found wherever ships have been used for war and trade–it still holds good, in principle, today. Warships can afford to be overmanned and of an uneconomically slender shape; a profit-making merchantman can not. The only occasion that the mania for speed overcame mercantile common-sense was in the middle of the nineteenth century, when the first American clippers were built for the San Francisco trade. These got longer and leaner and faster and needed larger crews to drive them until, in about fifteen short years, they priced themselves out of the market.

The Phoenicians sailed from their rich cities of Tyre, Carthage and Cadiz to the ends of the known world–and possibly beyond it. King Hiram of Tyre provided the material for King Solomon's temple: 'I will do all thy desire concerning timber of cedar . . . My servants shall bring them down from Lebanon unto the sea.' Later the two kings went into partnership and traded with Tarshish in Spain and Ophir in southern Arabia. The Phoenicians went north and traded in Brittany and Cornwall and may

possibly have ventured as far as the Baltic.

Going south, they had established a trading post at Cape Blanco–500 miles south of the Canaries–and had explored the West African coast as far as Cape Verde by 450 BC. Herodotus has it that Necho of Egypt sent a fleet manned by Phoenicians from the Red Sea, round the Cape of Good Hope and back to Egypt by the Straits of Gibraltar in about 600 BC, thus anticipating Vasco da Gama by some two thousand years. This is unsupported by any evidence but does show that in 400 BC Herodotus was aware that it was possible to go round the tip of Africa by sea.

By the time of the Roman Empire the design of merchantmen had stabilised into a form that would not really look out of place for the next thirteen hundred years. The grain ships of the Empire were broad, full-bodied, round-bottomed ships finer forward and fuller aft–rather like an avocado pear–with a mainmast towering 80 feet above the deck, supported by shrouds at the sides and stays running forward and backward. They also bore a new invention, a small raked mast forward carrying the 'artemon' or foresail, which helped the helmsman keep the ship on course.

These ships ran up to a hundred and eighty feet long, were some fifty feet in beam and drew in the region of twelve feet of water. It was in such a ship that Saint Paul was travelling when he was shipwrecked on the island of Malta. Their construction was of carvel planking (that is edge-to-edge, not

11

overlapping) on a framework of keel, stem- and stern-posts, ribs, and beams. The planks were joined together edgewise by wooden tongues let into both planks and then fastened with bronze nails. This form of construction can be seen in the 'Blackfriars ship', discovered when digging the foundations of County Hall, now the offices of the Greater London Council on the south bank of the Thames.

Having developed this practical and competent merchant craft, the Romans seem to have restricted themselves to navigating the Mediterranean. They obviously preferred dry land under their feet when they went a-conquering and relied on the Levantine traders for the carriage of exotica from distant lands to the markets which supplied the tables of Rome.

On the other side of the world, in the Pacific, men were also using the sea for trade and war, travelling the most incredible distances first on the great rafts with which Thor Heyerdahl has made us familiar and later in double canoes or vessels like the frameless 'prau' of Java. These latter were about fifty feet in length and only thirteen feet broad; they had two short masts, each carrying a curious low, long-nosed sail. They were still in evidence to greet the European adventurers when they arrived in those distant waters in the sixteenth century.

A curious vessel was developed in New Guinea—the 'lakatoi'—which consisted of three or more dug-

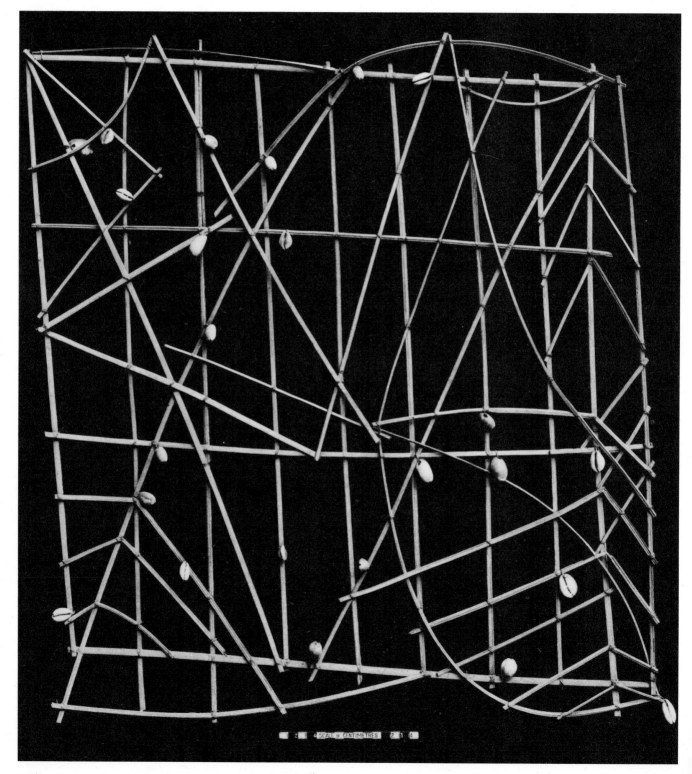

outs joined together by cross-beams. These multi-hulls carried a broad platform across the hulls for cargo and passengers and were driven by the distinctive claw-shaped sails that were found all over the Pacific.

The Pacific islanders developed a flourishing trade between islands many hundreds of miles apart using, for navigation, not only the sun and the stars but also the colour of the sea, the presence of currents and wave-systems, the direction of bird flight, and even the kind of fish and seaweed caught on their hooks. All this information was woven into maps of reeds, sticks and shells and preserved without the need of a written language.

Opposite: A Marshall Islands' map of reeds, sticks, and shells. Maps like this, woven apparently arbitrarily, do in fact give the Pacific navigator an adequate picture of currents, wave patterns, winds, and islands. Science Museum, London.

Left: Javanese sailing ships. 1–4 include a plan, aft elevation and section of a Batavian merchant ship; 5–9 a plan, aft elevation and forward and aft outrigger sections of a bedouang prao from Bezouki. *Essai sur la Construction Navale des Peuples Extra-Européens* edited by Arthus Bertrand, Paris. British Museum, London.

Chapter two
The Mediterranean & the Baltic

Twin centres of evolution

If you give two people an identical practical problem to solve they will, almost certainly, come up with very similar solutions; the only differences will probably be related to the different materials employed. This proposition certainly applies to boats: they have to be 'boat-shaped' no matter whether the builder is Samoan or Scandinavian. Thus, in Northern Europe, in contrast to the Mediterranean civilizations, the earliest boats were dug-outs, for use in sheltered waters, and boats made of hides sewn together and stretched over wooden frames, for the open sea. That this latter method will produce a sea-worthy boat cannot be doubted by anyone who has seen the West of Ireland curraghs or the Tristan da Cunha long-boats. The dug-outs were gradually improved by stitching extra planks along the sides to enlarge and deepen the hull. Each plank overlapped the one below and they were drilled and sewn together with hide – this overlapping technique being now known as 'clinker building' as opposed to the smooth carvel hulls of the Mediterranean craft.

These two methods of boat building, dug-out and skin-and-frame, gradually combined and complemented one another. The dug-out hull lengthened and narrowed into the keel and the stitched clinker planking was built up on a sound framework of stem- and stern-posts, ribs, and beams. The Hjortspring boat, found on the Danish island of Als and dating back to about 200 BC, is of this type of construction. She is some forty-four feet long and seven feet wide, and built of five overlapping planks attached to solid bow and stern pieces and supported by nine sets of ribs and beams. The centre plank is not yet differentiated as a keel proper. By the sixth century AD Scandinavian shipbuilding had developed the traditional 'Viking' ship, with a definite keel, ribs, beams and clinker planking. An interesting thing about these early ships is that the planking was attached to the framework by lashings and not by nails; this meant that the ship was flexible and able to alter somewhat in shape to suit the seas. It also allowed a lighter form of construction than would have been needed had these elegant and wicked-looking ships been entirely rigid.

In shape the Norse ships were both extremely graceful and extremely practical: a broad, flat centre-section, like the bowl of a champagne 'saucer', flowing easily to the long, slim, upcurved bow and stern. As in the Mediterranean, two types of ship were developed for the two basic purposes of trade and war. The merchant ships, which needed sailing ability with a small crew rather than speed and manoeuvrability under oars, extended the stem into a deep cutwater reminiscent of the Cretan Bronze Age traders. These ships were always steered with a single rudder pivoted on the right, or starboard (steerboard), side. The left-hand side of a ship, the port side, is so called because sailors naturally moored alongside a quay or port with the fragile rudder on the outside.

During the seventh and eighth centuries, these ships enlarged and developed into massive sea-going vessels eighty to ninety feet long and twenty feet broad, capable of sailing almost anywhere in the world. A replica of the ship found at Gokstad near Sandefjord in 1880 was sailed across the Atlantic in twenty-eight days in 1892. The Gokstad ship is 76 feet 5 inches from stem to stern, but some of the fighting long ships, or 'drakkars', of the Norsemen ran up to a hundred and fifty feet in length and were manned by eighty oarsmen. A feature of the Northern ships was their ability to make to windward under sail – a necessity in those waters where the winds are fickle in direction from day to day. It was ships like these that ferried Duke William of Normandy across the Channel in 1066, and they are shown on the Bayeux tapestry in all their finery of painted topsides, coloured sails and decorated stem- and stern-posts, carrying their cargo of men and horses to the conquest of England.

As national boundaries evolved in Europe and prosperity grew with the new-found stability, so trade developed enormously round the shores of the North Sea and the Baltic. Commercial interests led towns and city-states to join together for mutual profit and defence. The most famous of these syndicates is probably the Hanseatic League, an association which, at one time, threatened to gather the whole of Northern European coastal trade into its power.

The expansion of sea-borne trade means the development of ships, and the traders of the Hanse towns needed a more efficient cargo vessel than was then available. So the Hanse 'cog' of the thirteenth century came into being. The cog, which is portrayed on the seals of the towns of Wismar and Hardewijk, was a deep-draughted, roomy vessel with two important innovations. It had straight stem- and

A small curragh off the west coast of Ireland. Rowing boats made of tarred canvas stretched over a light wooden frame are still in use in all weathers off the rocky coasts of Eire. This method of construction was employed in early Northern sea-going boats.

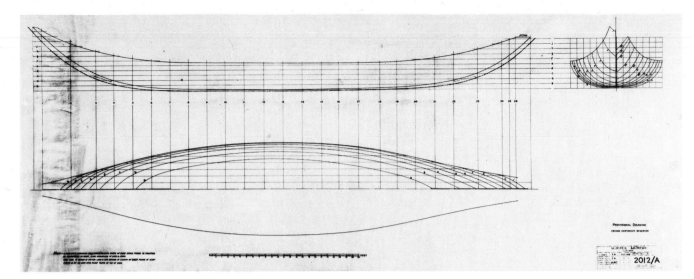

stern-posts and a stern rudder. The straight stem and stern ran down to a long straight keel and this, together with its deep draught, gave it much better sailing and sea-keeping qualities than the shallow, round-ended vessels still in use in England at that time. The Hanse merchants even moved whole estuary towns further down-river towards the sea to enable them to take advantage of this development— which gives some measure of the importance of the shipping trade at this period.

Trade in the Middle Ages was literally a cut-throat business, as exemplified in the illustration of a sea battle between merchant ships in the Bishop of Uppsala's *Historia de Gentibus Septentrionalibus* (History of the Scandinavians). Another example of the robust character of mediaeval trade is contained in an 'Agreement made betweene King Henrie the Fourth and the common societie of the Marchants of the Hans', published in Hakluyt's *English Voyages,* in which it was 'appointed, concluded and agreed' that the merchants of the King and of the Hanse 'from hencefoorth for one whole yeere and seven moneths immediately next ensuing and following, shall be permitted and licensed . . . to exercise mutual traffic, and, like marchants, to buy and sell together.' The greater part of the document is taken up by a list of grievances. For example: 'That about the feast of Easter 1394 Henry van Pomeren, Godekin Micheal and many others with them of Wismar and Rostok tooke, by maine force a ship of Newcastle on Tine . . .'; 'Item, in the yeere of our Lorde 1398 one John van Derlowe, Hans van Gelder, Clays Schelde, Everade Pilgrim and divers others . . . did villainously and unjustly take a shippe of John Wisedome of Hull called the *Trinitie';* and so on for some thirty articles stretching over ten years. The allegations were not all one sided for the League demanded recompense to be made to the inhabitants of Prussia, Livonia and other territories and cities of the Hanse for 'the injuries, damages and grievances unjustly done and committed against them by the subjects of the saide soveraigne lord the king.' It is curious to note that the alleged Hanse malefactors are identified by name while the English appear to have remained anonymous. Perhaps this is an early example of chauvinistic editing.

The first of the British Navigation Acts, later versions of which were to have a considerable effect

Opposite and below: The lines in the draught of the sixth-century Saxon burial ship at Sutton Hoo (Science Museum, London) are very similar to those of the seventh-century Gokstad war ship (Universitetets Oldsaksamling, Oslo). In both the flow is long, smooth, and in some way inevitable. Contemporary merchantmen were similar but broader in relation to their length.

Left: The Hanse cog on the Seal of Stralsund, 1329, has the same northern construction of overlapping planking as the Sutton Hoo and Gokstad ships, but it is pure merchant vessel. The seal clearly shows the straight stem and stern and less vulnerable central rudder. Staatsarchiv, Hamburg.

Opposite top: An Egyptian sailing ship, dating from the reign of Amenophis II (1450–1425 BC). A single steering oar performed the function of a rudder during this period. Grave of Sennofer, Thebes.

Opposite bottom: A detail from the Bayeux tapestry. The shipbuilders wielding axe and adze to shape the hulls and spars used in the Norman conquest of England are employing a method of construction which originated among the Vikings. Musée de la Reine Mathilde, Bayeux.

Below: The story of Saint Nicholas by Gentile da Fabriano (1370–1427). The squareness of a carrack's fore- and after-castle and its relative beaminess are emphasized in this painting. Pinacoteca Vaticana.

on ship design and construction, was passed in the reign of Richard II. These acts limited the carriage of goods into English ports to English ships or to ships belonging to the country of origin of the merchandise. Their objects were both to encourage English traders and to limit the power of the ship-owning middlemen of the great trading leagues. The operation of such a law at this period proved impracticable and, while the English, with their old-fashioned, round-bowed, shallow ships, held their own in the coastal trade, it was not until the sixteenth century that they were able successfully to compete for the richer prizes.

In 1383 Dom Fernando, the last of the Burgundian kings of Portugal, was succeeded by his bastard half-brother Dom João–Grand Master of the Order of Aviz. Dom João, after his accession, married Philippa, daughter of John of Gaunt. She bore him, among others, the Infante Dom Henrique, Grand Master of the Order of Christ, Duque de Vizeu–known to the world as Henry the Navigator.

This prince was informed with an insatiable desire to enlarge man's knowledge of the world about him, and was particularly interested in the exploration of the west coast of Africa. To give himself elbow-room,

and the atmosphere within which to work, he retired to the promontory of Sagres in the Algarve, where he built a fortress, an observatory, churches, houses and a dockyard. He founded there a school of navigation and attracted astronomers, mathematicians, cartographers and cosmographers from the whole of Europe. During his lifetime the Atlantic islands of Madeira, Porto Santo, the Azores and the Cape Verde Islands were all discovered and charted. The coast of Africa was opened up as far south as Sierra Leone. The next two hundred years–fitting curiously neatly with the Aviz dynasty–saw the Portuguese navigators spread south and then east around the globe. The Portuguese merchant adventurers, in search of precious metals, silks and, in particular, spices, established fortified harbours and trading posts on all the offshore islands of Africa, on the coasts and islands of the Indian Ocean, on the Malay peninsular at Malacca and as far east as Macao and Japan. By the middle of the sixteenth century most of the world had been opened up and quite accurately charted. These developments in cartography were in great part due to the innovations and improvements in instruments and mathematical techniques which

· COLONIA ·

Right: A battle between merchantmen, an illustration from *Historia de Gentibus Septentrionalibus,* Olaus Magnus, 1555. These vigorous traders both have the transom stern that was introduced in the sixteenth century.

Below: The port of Colonia, an illustration from the *Nuremberg Chronicle,* H. Schedel, 1493. This picture of a mediaeval port shows a typical carvel-planked round-ended ship of the fifteenth century.

The roads off Antwerp, *circa* 1518–40, by an unknown artist. A very busy port with caravels, spritsailed coasters and a lateen galley helped along by her oars. Nationaal Scheepvaartmuseum, Antwerp.

came from Henry's school of navigation at Sagres.

What sort of ships did these seamen sail? Here you come upon one of the classical problems of maritime history: no one, at any period, ever seems to have laid down an agreed nomenclature for types of sailing vessels. This is partly due to the fact that most books about ships or voyages are written by non-sailors to whom a 'frail bark (barque?)' is a poetic way of describing anything from a canoe to a full-rigged ship and who would call a cutter a barquentine for the sake of euphony. However, the early Portuguese navigators probably called their boats 'caravels' and they were almost certainly carvel-built (smooth planked), as were all Mediterranean ships of the period, and had two or three masts with a triangular 'lateen' sail on each. These fore-and-aft sails would have been essential for their return journey up the coast of Africa against the north-east trades. (There is an Arab proverb which declares that 'Only a madman or Christian sails against the wind'.)

A Portuguese manuscript of 1255 uses the word *caravela* to describe fishing vessels, and the few contemporary pictures from charts and altar-pieces show craft that look more like ships' boats than ships themselves. However, these tiny boats were in many ways well suited to voyages of exploration, being handy, capable of windward work and shallow-draughted to explore the shoals of coasts and

ARCHA·NOB
habitacio hoīm

...ialiū ...nunū in minu aialuum

...barum Apothera specierum

Stercoraria

rivers. The form of the caravel is still with us in the 'frigata', which can be seen on the Tagus. They are long, narrow boats with a fine entry and flaring bows which run back to long clean quarters and a square transom stern.

On Columbus's historic voyage across the Atlantic the two smaller vessels of his fleet – the *Niña* and the *Pinta* – were caravels whereas the flag-ship, the *Santa Maria,* was almost certainly a 'carrack'. Here again we come across the problem of terminology because Columbus himself only calls her the 'ship' as opposed to her two consort 'caravels'. Columbus actually disliked the *Santa Maria* because she was slow, more difficult to manoeuvre than his 'beloved *Niña*', of too great a draught and 'not suited for voyages of discovery'. This has not prevented her from becoming perhaps the most famous ship in the world. The most famous ship perhaps, but one about which practically nothing is known because no contemporary ever bothered to describe her. However, from a knowledge of ships of the period and from a knowledge of her complement and capacity, it is now generally agreed that she must have been some eighty feet in length, twenty-six feet in beam and have drawn about seven feet. We do know what sails she could carry because Columbus's log for 24 October, 1492, says: 'I let them set all sails, the main course with two bonnets, the fore course, the spritsail, the mizzen, the topsail and the boat's sail on the half deck.' With this lot set and drawing she probably rushed through the water at nearly eight miles an hour. The lines of the *Santa Maria* are wholly unknown and all that one can be sure of is that most museum models made before the Second World War are wrong. A lot of these models were based on a Portuguese 'replica' sailed across the Atlantic in 1892 in a time of thirty-six days. During her crossing the replica achieved a speed of 6½ knots and there is a laconic report that 'The vessel pitched horribly.' Her underwater shape was really quite unsuitable for a small square-rigged sailing ship, but the most glaring error was the shape of the stern: the transom stern was not used in ships of this type until well into the sixteenth century and the *Santa Maria* was not a new ship when she sailed in 1492.

The first English expedition to America was made five years later, in 1497, by John Cabot. 'This year on St John the Baptist's day [24 June] the land of America was found by the Merchants of Bristow in a shippe of Bristow called the *Mathew;* the which ship departed from the port of Bristowe the second day of May and came home again the 6th of August next following.'

John Cabot had been granted letters patent by Henry VII in March of the previous year, and these show the king to be a very careful business man. 'The King, to all to whom, etc. Greeting: Be it known and made manifest that we have given and granted as by these presents we give and grant, . . . to our well-beloved John Cabot, citizen of Venice, and to Lewis, Sebastian and Sancio, sons of the said John . . . power to sail to all parts, regions and coasts of the eastern, western and northern sea, under our banners, flags and ensigns, with five ships or vessels of whatsoever burden and quality they may be . . . at their own proper cost and charges . . . in such a way nevertheless that of all the fruits, profits, emoluments, commodities, gains and revenues accruing from this

voyage . . . to pay us, either in goods or money, the fifth part of the whole capital gained . . .'

A household book of Henry VII transcribed by Craven Ord in the nineteenth century carries the following entries which show the king's interest in exploration:

		£	s.	d.
f.41 12 Hen. VII,	Aug 10 To hym that founde the new Isle	10	0	0
f.44 13 Hen. VII,	Jan 1st To a Venysian in rewarde		66	8
f.45 13 Hen. VII,	March 22 To Lanslott Thirkill of London apon a prest for his Shipp going towards the new Ilande	20	0	0
Ibid (same date)	Delivered to Launcelot Thirkill going towards the new Ile in Prest	20	0	0
Ibid 13 Hen. VII,	Apr 1st To Thomas Bradley and Launcelott Thirkill going to the new Isle	30	0	0
f.45b (same date)	To John Carter going to the New Isle, in reward		40	0

26

Left: The port of Hamburg, an illustration from the *Hamburger Stadtrecht,* 1497. The ships lying at anchor show the straight stern-posts introduced by the Hanse shipwrights three hundred years earlier. Staatsarchiv, Hamburg.

Below: Portuguese carracks off a rocky coast, 1530, by Cornelis Anthoniszoon. A busy scene with men manning the yards while manoeuvring close inshore and galleys rowing to windward and running downwind. National Maritime Museum, Greenwich.

However, not all the voyages of exploration were profitable, as this extract from the London Chronicle (*Cronicon regum Anglie*) shows: 'This yere the kyng at the besy request and supplicacion of a Straunger venisian, which by a Caart made hym self expert in knowyng of the world, caused the kyng to manne a ship with vytaill & other necessaries for to seche an Iland wheryn the said straunger surmysed to be grete comodities. With which ship by the kynges grace so rygged went iij or iiij [3 or 4] moo owte of Bristowe, the said straunger being Conditor of the said fflete. Wheryn dyvers merchaunts as well of london as Bristow aventured goodes & sleight merchaundises, which departed from the west cuntrey in the begynnyng of somer, but to this present moneth came nevir knowledge of their exployt.'

Henry VIII also sent ships out to explore the coasts of North America. John Rut wrote a letter to the Honourable King's Grace of England in 'bad English and worse Writing' in which he tells of the voyage of the *Mary of Gilford* and the loss of the *Samson,* of how on their venturing north they came upon great islands of ice and the mainland was 'all wildernesse and mountaines and woods, and no naturall ground but all mosse, and no inhabitation nor no people in [those] parts: and in the woods [they] found footing of divers great beasts, but [they] saw none.' After the loss of the *Samson* they sailed south again to the island of San Juan where they found 'eleven saile of Normans, and one Brittaine, and two Portugall Barkes, and all a-fishing'. John Rut makes the voyage sound very peaceful and innocent but a Spanish description of the same voyage begins: 'In the year 1527 an English corsair, under the pretext that he was going to discover, came with a great ship in the direction of Brazil [This is the mythical Isle of Brazil of the ancients. P.J.B.] on the coast of Tierra Firme.' On his arrival in Santo Domingo and his request to trade with the Spanish, Rut was promptly fired upon and forced to retire to the more friendly inhabitants of San Juan.

Chapter three
The development of navigation

By the sixteenth century the greater part of the earth's surface had been explored, or, more correctly, the majority of the world's seas had been sailed, and sea-going vessels had been voyaging to the expanding limits of their world for nearly three thousand years. And all of this was done without the benefit of what a modern mariner would regard as the basic necessities for successful navigation. So how did the earliest seamen find their way about their seas, and how were the demands of merchants and the outward urge of the adventurers met by the ever-increasing skills of the astronomer and of the mathematician?

Originally, seamanship was a trade and a mystery and it was approached through a long, hard apprenticeship. The simple answer to the question 'How did a Phoenician or a Cretan or a Norseman know where he was without chart or compass?' is that he had been there before. He had been there

many times before during his apprenticeship and was trained to remember the shape of a headland, the set of a current, the wave pattern where two currents met and even the colour of the water where it changed at the mouth of a distant river or over the shallows of a shoal.

The lack of compass, sextant and chronometer did not, however, mean that all sense of position and direction were lacking. The sun has always appeared to rise in the east, swing round through south and set in the west (at least in the northern hemisphere). The Pole Star has remained relatively fixed in the heavens, while the other constellations circle the sky. The winds themselves are variable in detail but are so recognizable in general pattern as to have been named from the earliest times. In Homer's *Odyssey*, Odysseus steered east for seventeen days following Calypso's sailing directions: 'It was [the Great Bear] that the wise Goddess had told him to keep to his left hand as he crossed the sea.'

The realization that the altitude of the Pole Star gave a clue to position also came very early. Lucan, writing in about AD 64, has a sailor end a short, but improving, lecture to the fugitive Pompey with the words: '. . . *propriorque mari Cynosura feretur, In Siriae Portus tendet ratis'*, which might be freely rendered as 'The nearer Cynosura [the Pole Star] drops towards the sea, the nearer we are to the Syrian port.' The Egyptians measured the height of the stars against a seated figure placed in a set relation to the observer and noted that a star was 'at his shoulder' or 'at his ear'. Due, probably, to the lack of reference books, men were much more interested in, and observant of, the world about them than they are today in this age of the "instant expert". For example, an Icelandic monk visiting the Holy Land in 1150 wrote: '. . . by Jordan, if a man lies down flat on the ground, raises his knee, places his fist upon it, and then raises his thumb from his fist he sees the Pole Star just so high and no higher.' The fact that stars can give both direction and latitude has been common knowledge among seamen for several thousand years.

The earliest "artificial" aids to navigation were sailing directions—originally written for the pilot's own benefit as an *aide-memoire*. Seaman's lore for the North African coast was collected in about 500 BC in the *Periplous of Scylax of Caryanda*. Starting at the mouth of the Nile and travelling westwards, this gives

Opposite: A mariner's astrolabe. This sixteenth-century astrolabe was found under a rock on Valencia (off the west coast of Ireland). At first it was thought to be Spanish – two wrecks from the Armada were close by – but recent scholarship now suggests that it is of English manufacture. National Maritime Museum, Greenwich.

Left: A chart of the West Indies and Florida from an atlas by Lazaro Luis, 1563. The chart shows the distortion of longitude to be expected before the invention of an accurate timepiece. Academia das Ciências, Lisbon.

Right top: A sextant by an unknown maker, *circa* 1770. National Maritime Museum, Greenwich.

Right bottom: The wooden midshipman, a chart publisher's sign described by Charles Dickens in *Dombey and Son*. The Dickens House, London, on loan from Imray, Laurie, Norrie & Wilson Limited, whose sign it was for two hundred years.

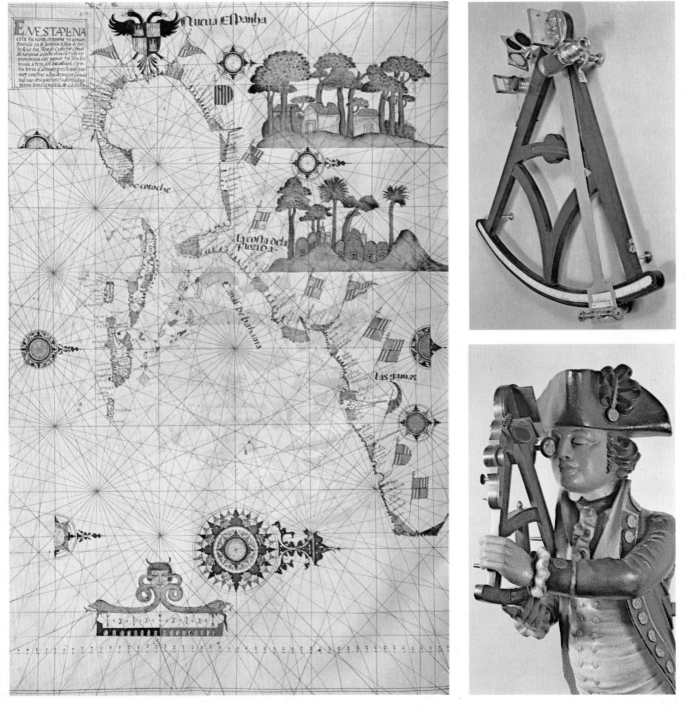

the following sort of information about the coast of
North Africa: 'Coasting from the Pillars of Hercules
to Cape Hermaea is two days; from Cape Hermaea to
Cape Soloeis is three days, and from Cape Soloeis to
Cerne is seven days' coasting. The parts beyond the
Isle of Cerne are no longer navigable, because of
shoals, mud and seaweed. The traders here are
Phoenicians.' A second early pilot-book, dating
probably from the third century AD, is the *Stadiasmus
of the Great Sea,* which covers much the same area in
greater detail. A typical entry from the section on
Crete reads: 'From Casus to Samnonium 300 stadia.
This is a promontory in Crete which extends far to
the North: there is a temple of Athene: it has an
anchorage and water.'

Neither of these two books gives any indication of
direction since they are concerned only with coasting
passages always in sight of land. For travelling out of
sight of land, however, some form of direction had to
be given to the reader. The prevailing winds were
used, and sailing directions were as follows: 'From
Paphos to Alexandria—3800 stadia with Boreas [the
north-east wind]', 'From Cyrene to Criumelopon—
2000 stadia with Leuconotus [a wind about SSW by
W]'. Timosthenes, a learned sailor who flourished
under Ptolemy II (285–46 BC), divided the 'wind rose'
into twelve parts of some thirty degrees each. This
was regarded as 'too subtle and meticulous' by most
sailors, according to Pliny, and the most common
division of the winds was into eight—later halved and
halved again into sixteen and thirty-two points or
'rhumbs'. The Temple of the Winds in Athens is an
octagonal building with a representation of the

appropriate wind on the appropriate face. Particular
winds were often named after their discoverer, as
were capes, islands and bays. The south-west monsoon
was called 'Hippalus' after a Greek shipmaster of that
name who was the first man to sail a ship across the
Indian Ocean direct to Malabar.

The knowledge required of a pilot in those
instrumentless times was well summarized in the
Sanskrit *Mu'allim* of AD 434. 'He knows the course of
the stars and can always orient himself; he knows the
value of signs, both regular, accidental and
abnormal, of good and bad weather; he distinguishes
the regions of the oceans by the fish, the colour of the
water, the nature of the bottom, the birds, the
mountains, and other indications.' And the only aids
that he possessed were his memory, helped perhaps by
a pilot-book, and a sounding line or staff.

The earliest mention of that item essential to a
modern navigator, the magnetic compass, is by an
English monk, a lecturer at Paris University in the
1180s, Alexander Neckham. In his *De Utensilibus* he
lists among a ship's stores '. . . a needle placed upon a
dart, and it is turned and whirled round until the
point of the needle looks North-East (sic). And so the
sailors know which way to steer when the Cynosura
is hidden by the clouds.' A little less than a hundred
years later in a comprehensive volume of sailing
directions for the Mediterranean and Black Seas—the
Compasso da Navigare—the sailing directions are
given in terms of the compass rose and not the wind
rose. So: 'First, from Cape Vincent to the mouth of
the river of Seville, 150 miles between East and
South-East . . . and if you wish to enter the river,

Le routier et pilotage

Sur la pointe qui fait lentree de saint martin deuers bas ya une tour bort a bort de la mer. Et icelle pointe auec la tour est de telle figure.

Et aual de saint martin et prez verras une pointe quant seras au bas de luy. laditte poite est sebable a ceste cy: et est au bas de saint martin.

Et aual de ceste poite verras une petite ance de sable: au bas delle sur la prochaine pointe verras une chapelle. Et en terre verras une tour deuers soest sur la pointe. Et puis verras une ance de sable plus grande et plus aual. et la prochaine pointe au bas delle: sera lentree de saint vincent celle deuers lhault et la pointe deuerslhault qui est toute pelee et est soubme a la mer.

Deuant lentree de sait vincet ya une petite isle et assez grade et et assez haulte. et le bout damont est le plus gros et le plus hault et est rond et va

De la mer.

m appointant deuers bas et au bout damont. et ya ung ferraillon. Et ya passee dun bort et dautre. La meilleure de gros teps et de grosse vas gue est deuer esoest de ceste isle nonobstat a la passee est bone en terre de luy de vent qui arriue en rangeant de luy. et est sebable a ceste figure.

Se tu atterres au bas de saint vincet: tu verras les trecheee de saint vincent qui sont au bas du haure et prez deluy qui est une terre bien trenchee comme morceaulx de sel par troys ou quatre lieux Et se te es au bas du haure: tu verras deux ferraillone comme deux petites isles qui sont a lentree deuers bas. Et ya passee entre terre et eulx et dun bort et dautre comme deuant est dit. Et se tu veulx entrer deuers est: range les ferraillone qui sont comme une isle et te demourront deuers le nort qui sera destreboit en entrat mais au dehors deulx ya une basse bien hors au bort deuers la mer. Et par ce baille leur bon ryn tusques a ce que soys par le dedens deulx et le trauers deulx se tu passes lest.

Se tu passes deuers soest de ceste isle que lon appelle lisle du ferraillon il est: range deuers soest. car il est le meilleur et ya renoc de vet doest sur la pointe deuers soest du haure saint vincent qui est bien grosse poin: te verras une chapelle.

Se tu atterres le trauers de luerg et est au bas de preup et ya huyt lieues dabilles tu verras une chapelle blanche qui est bort a bort de la mer et amont delle et prez: et verras une pointe. Et ne verras point dautre chapelle que celle de entre luerque et ribedoe.

De luerque et ribedoe ya huyt lieues.

Se tu atterres le trauers de ribedoe: tu verras motegue qui est une montaigne haulte Et se tu es le trauers delle: tu verras haulte sur lautre terre: et verras sur elle ung tel groing nault come ceste figure qui sensuit.

---

beware of the bank called Zizar to the West.' This form will be very familiar to any sailor nowadays: it is indistinguishable from any modern pilot. In 1483 a French sailor, Pierre Garcie, published his *Grant Routier et Pilotage,* the first published 'rutter' to carry woodcuts of prominent headlands and land-marks. The Breton tide charts were a further advance dating from this period. These gave the time of high water at full moon and new moon for the major ports from Finisterre to Flanders.

While Pierre Garcie and Brouscon le Breton were compiling their rutters and tide tables as practical aids to mariners, the cosmographers were re-discovering the *Geography* of Ptolemy. This was to prove of the utmost importance because Ptolemy imposed upon his maps a grid system of parallels of latitude and meridians of longitude. It was taken up

by the fifteenth-century cartographers and navigators and, for the first time, maps became relatively accurate–at least in so far as latitude was concerned; longitude was to remain a problem for the next three hundred years. In 1420 Henry the Navigator sent for the brilliant instrument-maker, cartographer and compass-maker, the elderly Jew, Master James of Majorca. He installed him in his university at Sagres to consider the navigational problems of the Portuguese explorers. By 1433 the Portuguese were finding their ports by measuring the sun's, or a star's, altitude, sailing north or south until this altitude matched that of the port they sought, and then turning and running down the latitude. This method of seeking the right latitude and then keeping to it is still used by cruising yachtsmen and space satellites today.

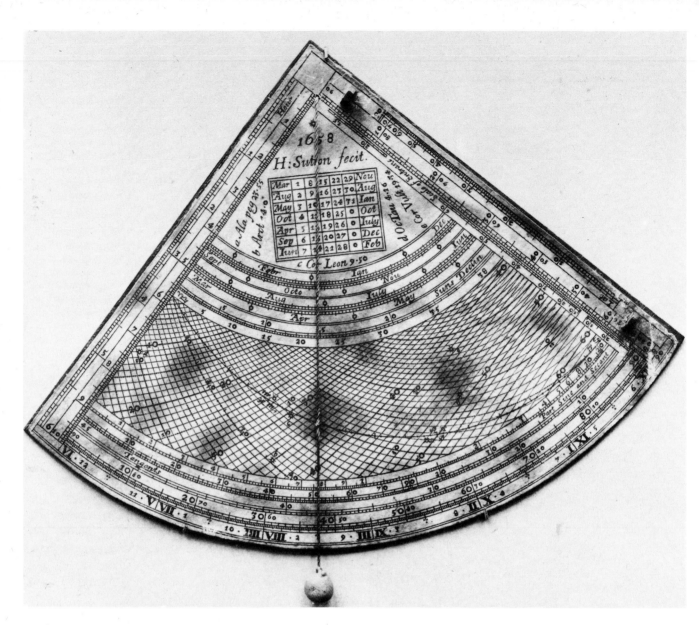

Two instruments were available to the fifteenth-century mariner for measuring the altitude of a heavenly body–the 'quadrant' and the 'astrolabe'. Both were originally designed for use on land by sophisticated astronomers and astrologers and were simplified and stripped to their bare essentials for use at sea.

The quadrant is an extremely simple instrument in its basic principles. It consists of a quarter of a circle with a pair of sights on one straight edge, a plumb bob suspended from the angle between the two radii and an arc marked off into ninety degrees–half a protractor, in fact. To use it, you held it up and lined up the sights with (say) the Pole Star. When you were on target you simply secured the plumb line so that it could not move and read off the angle that the vertical made on the scale. Since the earliest users were ignorant of geometry and understood neither the functions of degrees nor the meaning of latitude, these quadrants were often marked only with the names of the headlands and ports at the relevant parts of the scale.

The mariner's astrolabe consisted of only the reverse of the astronomer's version, which was a very sophisticated instrument indeed. It was simply a heavy brass disc with an 'alidade' or sighting arm

pivoting about the centre and two vanes with pin holes attached to the alidade as sights; the circumference was engraved with a scale of degrees. In use the astrolabe was suspended by its thumb-ring –usually by an assistant–and the sun's elevation was measured by rotating the alidade until the light passed through both the pin holes in the sight vanes. For star sights the mariner looked directly through a larger pair of holes in the vanes. As can be imagined, it was an extremely difficult instrument to use on the heaving deck of a ship in a seaway and was therefore normally used on shore, the navigator solemnly putting ashore in a ship's boat, making his observations and returning to the ship.

The Arabs, who led the world in mathematics and navigation at this time, developed an extremely simple instrument for measuring the altitude of a heavenly body –the 'kamal'. This consisted of a wooden rectangle attached in the centre to a length of knotted string. By putting the free end of the string in one's mouth and holding the tablet so that its base seemed to rest on the horizon when the string was extended, different pre-arranged angles could be subtended, depending on which knot was held between the teeth. A European development of the kamal was the 'cross-staff'–first used in Europe by

Opposite: A quadrant, signed by H. Sutton, 1658. This example of perhaps the simplest celestial instrument carries a bewildering amount of information. Rule-of-thumb versions were available for less literate sailors. Science Museum, London.

Below: A universal ring dial by Edmund Culpeper (1660–1730). The instrument was used to measure the sun's altitude at noon. The accuracy with which early instruments were engraved is beautifully illustrated by this example of Culpeper's work. Science Museum, London.

An eighteenth-century nocturnal. It was
used to read the pointers of the Great Bear
like the hour hand of a clock.
Nederlandsch Historisch Scheepvaart
Museum, Amsterdam.

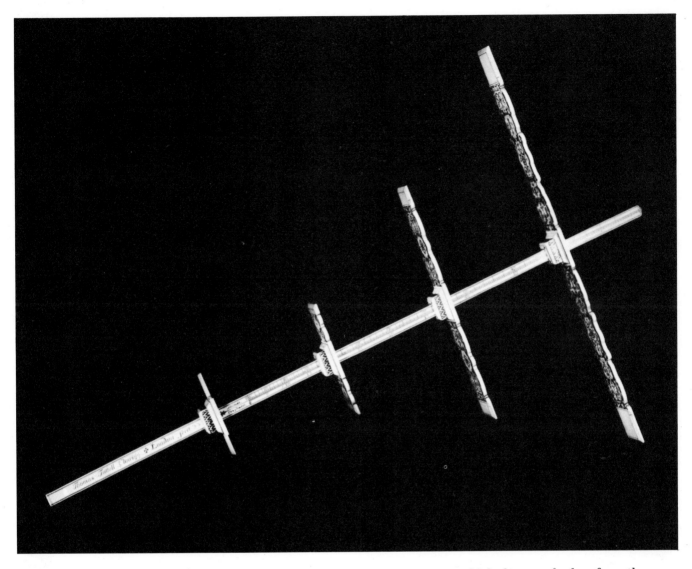

Vasco da Gama's pilot in 1498. This was a simple graduated rod with a number of variously sized movable cross-pieces running on it; the rod was held to the eye and the suitable cross-piece was adjusted back and forth until it exactly occupied the space between the horizon and the sun, the other pieces meanwhile being removed from the rod.

The snag with these two instruments was that the observer had to look directly at the sun, which was both uncomfortable and inaccurate; he had also simultaneously to observe the horizon, which was difficult. Partly to overcome these problems and partly to make actual manipulation of the instrument easier, John Davis developed and improved the 'back-staff'. He sailed under Captain Lancaster as pilot on the first voyage of the Honourable East India Company in 1601 so he was familiar with the problem of trying to look at both sun and sea at once in the tropics, where the sun is nearly directly overhead. When using the back-staff, the observer turned his

back on the sun, which threw a shadow from the vane on the upper quadrant on to an ivory reflector. The horizon and this shadow were then aligned through the sight on the lower quadrant.

This was still a cumbersome instrument to use on board a rolling ship, and it was not until 1731 that John Hadley demonstrated his new 'octant' to his fellow members of the Royal Society, claiming for his invention that it was possible to use it accurately '. . . though the ship rolls ever so much . . . and the Observer has the same Advantage of making the Observation as if he took it in smooth Water . . .' This octant is the direct fore-runner of the modern sextant, which works on the identical principle. The image of the observed body is reflected down on to a half-mirrored, half-plain reflector, through the plain portion of which the horizon is simultaneously observed. Speaking from personal experience, although the sextant is an excellent instrument to use, even in a seaway, I think that John Hadley

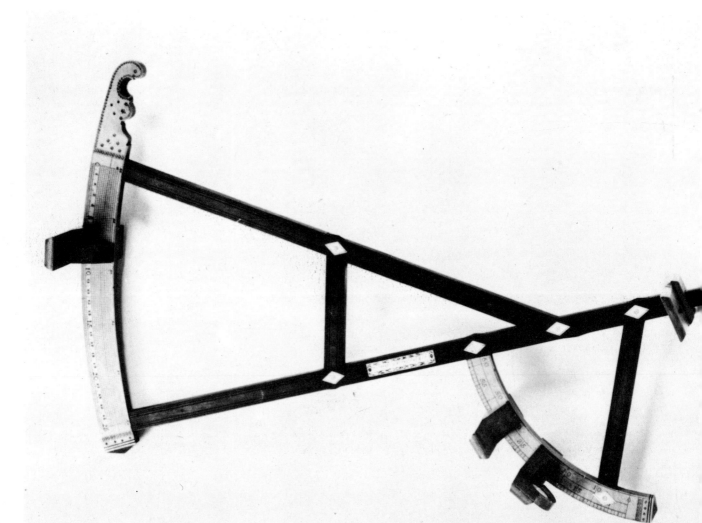

somewhat overstated his case. Still, by the middle of the eighteenth century the problem of finding latitude accurately had been solved. But this is only half of what is involved in determining position.

'Dead reckoning' is the most basic form of navigation, and it is, paradoxically, now incorporated in the most sophisticated inertial systems for atomic submarines. Quite simply, you are using dead reckoning when you reason thus: 'I started from A; I have travelled 30 miles due north and I have been set two miles due east by the tide. I must therefore be at B.' Over shortish distances and where the effects of tides and currents are known, this is quite a satisfactory method of navigation. However, where unknowns are allowed to multiply, gross errors are

soon apparent. To use dead reckoning two things are needed: an accurate sense of direction and distance. Direction was given by the sun, the stars or the wind or compass rose. Distance was given by the multiplication of speed by time. With experience, the speed could be guessed – with surprising accuracy – or measured by the use of some specially designed instrument. The 'ship's log and line' is first mentioned in the 1590s. This consisted of a piece of wood so attached to a line as to lie across the pull and cause maximum drag; the line was knotted every seven fathoms (or 42 feet). The log was cast overboard, the line allowed to run, a half-minute sand-glass turned, and the number of knots which ran out during its span counted. The number of knots gave the ship's

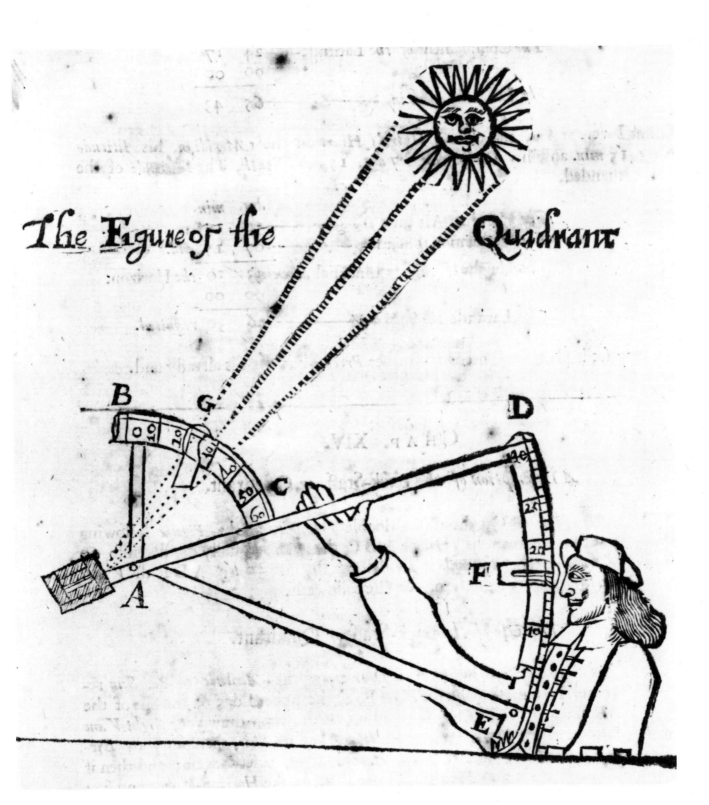

This contemporary wood-cut from *The Mariner's Magazine,* Captain Samuel Sturmy, 1669, shows how John Davis's new instrument was used.

The Figure of the Quadrant

speed in miles per hour (so 'knot'=rate of motion).

Two other sizes of sand-glass had been in common use at sea from the eleventh century onwards: the watch-glass, which measured a four-hour watch and stood some two feet high, and the half-hour glass. These crude time-pieces, plus the later half-minute glass, and the sun and the stars were the only means the navigator had of telling the time–and time is essential to the navigator because, as latitude is given by the difference in altitude, so longitude is given by difference in time. Longitude, so far as seamen were concerned, was always a matter of informed guesswork until the middle of the eighteenth century. For the land-based astronomer it was possible to calculate the hour-angle, or longitude, of observatories by means of eclipses of the sun, transits

of planets and other such predictable astronomical phenomena; the seaman relied on dead reckoning and the rule of thumb.

Thirty years after Hadley had demonstrated the octant, another John, John Harrison, claimed the award from the Board of Longitude for the invention of the first successful chronometer. This 'Chronometer Number Four' was so accurate that, after a passage to the West Indies lasting eighty-one days, the error was only 5·1 seconds of time–or about one sixtieth of a degree of longitude. Shortly afterwards Nevil Maskeleyne published his *Nautical Almanac,* and the sailor had, at last, all the instruments and information necessary for finding his position at sea without any reference to known and visible landmarks.

Opposite left: An octant, *circa* 1750, by an unknown maker. Invented by John Hadley in 1731, it made the simultaneous observation of the sun and horizon a much less uncomfortable exercise – by the introduction of a half-mirrored, half-plain reflector. Science Museum, London.

Opposite right: A ship's log in the shape of a fish. A line knotted every seven fathoms would have been attached to it. The ship's log and line was used to determine the speed at which a vessel was travelling. Science Museum, London.

Below: Harrison's first chronometer, 1735. Twenty-six years and three chronometers after the production of this superb piece of machinery John Harrison successfully claimed the Board of Longitude's award for an accurate marine timepiece. National Maritime Museum, Greenwich, on loan from the Ministry of Defence (Navy).

Chapter four
The exploitation of the Indies

As the fifteenth and sixteenth centuries saw the greatest strides in maritime discovery, with the opening of the sea routes to India and China, the circumnavigation of the globe by Magellan and Drake and the discovery of the Americas, so the seventeenth and eighteenth centuries saw the expansion and development of trade and empire which had been made possible by the early explorers. Trade follows the flag and exploitation inevitably follows exploration – in the 1970s a group of businessmen want to follow the American and Russian space programmes and turn the moon to profit.

The three great East India companies were all founded in the seventeenth century: the British in 1600, the Dutch in 1602, and the French company in 1664. West India companies were incorporated at much the same time, and the Company of Gentlemen Adventurers of Hudson's Bay was granted its charter in 1670. The great trading companies soon became inextricably entangled in foreign and domestic politics, and new companies were even founded for purely political reasons – for example the disastrous South Sea Company, which was brought into being by the Tory Party to try to balance the enormous financial power of the Whig-dominated first and second East India companies.

This development of trade involved the acquisition of territory by treaty, alliance and plain conquest and the defence of those territories against the attacks of company rivals, and it required a new breed of merchant ship. It is difficult to know whether to describe the company ships as armed merchantmen or cargo-carrying warships. In fact these well-found ships, manned by well-fed and well-paid volunteer crews, were a match for almost any warship of similar tonnage. Armament was essential when you consider that the English, French, Dutch and Spanish were almost continually at war for the whole of the seventeenth and eighteenth centuries.

However, before discussing the ships used in the Atlantic and Pacific trade it would be as well to consider the Dutch 'fluyt', which dominated European trade to such an extent that it could almost be regarded as the cause of the Anglo-Dutch wars of the mid-seventeenth century. The Dutch had over 10,000 merchantmen in service at the beginning of the century, and over half the Baltic trade, controlled by the customs at Elsinore, was carried in Dutch ships.

Left: The first page of the charter granted to the Company of Gentlemen Adventurers of Hudson's Bay on 2 May 1670. Hudson's Bay Company, London.

Below: A Dutch East Indiaman (*right*), 1647, by Wensel Hollar. This well-armed plump merchantman being towed by her boats in a calm epitomizes the self-sufficient attitude of the East India companies. Museum Plantin-Moretus en Prentenkabinet, Antwerp.

Mercatoria Hollandica, per Indias Orientales

Below: A Dutch merchant ship, 1647, by Wensel Hollar. Built for the European trade, it contrasts with the East Indiamen in its lack of armament and smaller crew. The Dutch were noted for building easy-to-handle ships to use their limited manpower economically. Museum Plantin-Moretus en Prentenkabinet, Antwerp.

Opposite top: An English merchantman, *Voyages and Explorations*, James Bolland, 1675. This print is titled 'An English Merchantman with all her sayles sett as here demonstrated'. Close-hauled on the port tack, she does not use her mizzen or bowsprit sails. Science Museum, London.

Opposite bottom: An English merchant pink (also called an English flute) off Satalia, 1677, by Jan Peeters. The round planking and high stern agree with Fredrik af Chapman's classification of hull shapes in his *Architectura Navalis Mercatoria*. National Maritime Museum, Greenwich.

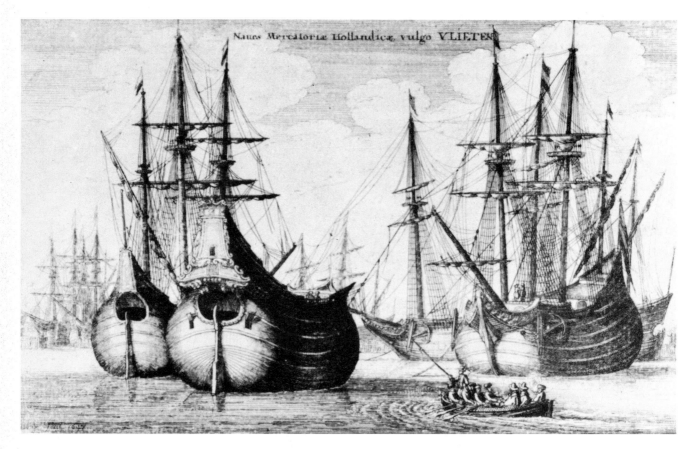

The fluyt was a flat-bottomed, round-sterned, rather narrow vessel running some hundred to one hundred and thirty feet long. The narrowness of the fluyt is an early example of the way in which government legislation affected ship design. The calculation of custom's duty at Elsinore – which controlled the Øresund, the narrow strait between Denmark and Sweden – was based on a measurement of tonnage which depended in a large part on the breadth of a ship amidships. This legislation was amended in 1669 and from then onwards fluyts were built progressively beamier.

Draughts of ships date from about the beginning of the seventeenth century and we do have a record of an early small Dutch merchantman of a different type from the fluyt. This is to be found in Joseph Fürttenbach's *Architectura Navalis*, which was published in 1629. It shows a long, narrow ship (the length about five times the beam) with a flat stern, a very flat bottom and a great degree of 'tumble home' (i.e. the sides of the ship slope inwards from above the waterline). This shape has several advantages: firstly, as with the fluyts, it decreased the customs' charges; secondly, narrow gun-decks meant that the centre of gravity was nearer the centre of the ship, which meant greater stability; and thirdly, when two such ships lay together in battle – and merchantmen not only carried teeth but used them – they touched at

the waterline but their deck railings were well out of jumping distance for a boarding party. Fürttenbach's ship is shown rigged with three masts, carrying courses (mainsails) and topsails on the foremast and mainmast and a triangular lateen sail on the mizzen, or aftermost mast. This last sail was used only as an aid to steering when going to windward. His illustration shows a row of gun ports on the main deck and four guns mounted in the well. The quarter and half decks are fully planked and there is a delightful Italianate shingle-roofed stern gallery. An interesting feature is the presence of a long beam lying across the 'beak-head'; the beak-head was the pointed, often decorated projection from the true bow of the ship which supported the bowsprit and carried the figurehead. This beam is the first appearance in a Dutch ship of a 'cat-head' (a beam from which purchases for stowing the anchor were slung). For some reason the Dutch always built their cat-heads from the beak-head whereas English and French shipwrights sprung theirs from the forecastle.

Another working drawing, dating from the latter part of the seventeenth century, shows a 'pinnace'. This was a small, ship-rigged vessel used in both trade and war. Unlike the fluyt, it had a flat, transom stern, a single deck carrying some seven guns and high, sweeping bulwarks giving a most attractive bold sheer. The Dutch traders were always very easily

A

Top: Whampoa anchorage, *circa* 1720, by W. T. Huggins. A busy Eastern anchorage with Indiamen at anchor, hove-to waiting clearance, and sailing homeward. City Museum and Art Gallery, Urban Council, Hong Kong.

Bottom: The plan of Fort George at Madras. This typical East India Company fort was built in 1640–forty years after the company's foundation. Most such 'factories' were built on islands or peninsulas for ease of defence.

Opposite: The artificial island of Deshima (*foreground*), for more than three hundred years the only European trading station in Japan. Foreign ships were not allowed to enter Nagasaki Bay under sail but were towed in by Japanese rowing boats. Nederlandsch Historisch Scheepvaart Museum, Amsterdam.

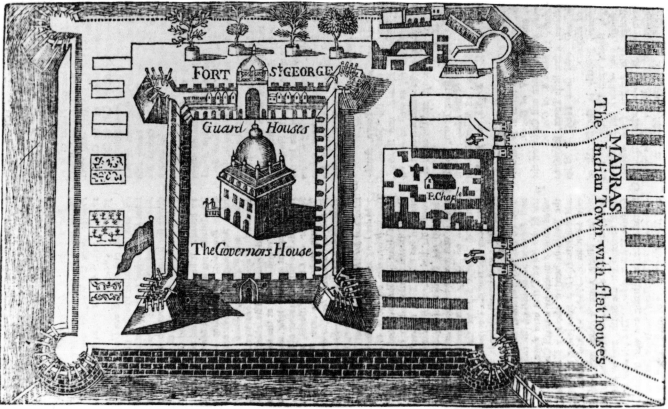

handled ships because the size of the Dutch merchant marine represented an enormous drain on manpower. Sir Walter Raleigh, in fact, complained bitterly in 1603 that, while a crew of ten could handle a Dutch ship of 100 tons, it took thirty men to manage an English ship of similar tonnage.

In the seventeenth and eighteenth centuries, which saw the foundation of the British and Dutch empires, the rise of colonial America and its successful struggle for independence, the liberation of the Spanish Netherlands and the French revolution, trade was dominated by the great trading companies. They had their own armies and navies; they built their own ships and owned their own shipyards and factories—and wrote long memoranda to themselves explaining why it was best that way. They formed alliances with foreign potentates, made treaties and waged war—all with a fine eye for profit. But often they also brought stability and justice to the territories they managed. It was not until 1785 that the British East India Company was brought under a measure of government control, and not until the disastrous Mutiny of 1858 that it was finally wound up.

The first Dutch East Indiamen were a direct result of Spanish political action. After the death of Henry of Portugal in 1580 and the seizure of the Portuguese crown by Philip II of Spain, the port of Lisbon was closed to the Dutch, who were just starting their fight against Spanish rule. Unable to trade with the Indies through the intermediary of the Portuguese, the Dutch were forced to send their own ships halfway round the world. In 1595 the States General sent out a fleet of four ships; three of them returned ladened with spices two years and four months later. They were fair-sized ships for their time, built on the long sweet lines of the galleon, three-masted, with square sails on the forward two masts and a lateen mizzen.

As I said earlier, the classification of ships always presents a problem; names were not exactly applied by contemporary writers and usages changed rapidly. In the eighteenth century it was more usual to differentiate ships by their hull shape than their rig. Fredrik Henrik af Chapman in his *Architectura Navalis Mercatoria*—published in 1768—divides merchantmen into five categories, mainly by details of their bow and stern shapes. 'Frigates', 'hagboats' and 'pinks' all had beak-heads, whereas the 'cat' and 'barque' had bluff, undecorated bows. Aft, the frigate had a transom and slight counter-stern, but the hagboat's planking was carried round to about the line of the main deck, and that of the pink was rounder still with a high, narrow stern. The cat was rather similar to the pink, whereas the barque had

The *Falmouth* by J. Hood. The lines of this
early Blackwall frigate should be compared
with those of the *Agamemnon* (page 93),
launched a hundred years later. National
Maritime Museum, Greenwich.

'The FALMOUTH Cap.tⁿ THO.ˢ FIELD Launch't at BLACKWALL the 14.ᵗʰ of August 1752 Length ⁿʳ Keel 108.9, Breadth 34, Burthen 668 §'

more of a counter—like the frigate. To cause more
confusion, any one of these hulls could carry the rig
associated with any of the others and be called by
either name. Nowadays it is usual to call a sailing
ship by the name of the rig it carries, irrespective of
the hull shape. This is a much easier system since
sails are easily recognizable in size, shape and
number, even at a distance.

However, most of the East Indiamen from the
eighteenth century were frigates by either classification. The *Falmouth,* built by John Perry of
Blackwall and launched in 1752, was 108 feet in the
keel with a 43-foot beam and a burthen of 668 tons.
She carried twenty-two guns on her main deck and
half-a-dozen lighter cannon on her poop deck. She
was rigged with square topsails and top-gallants on
all three masts, square courses on the foremast and
mainmast and a fore-and-aft gaff mizzen. She also
carried a square spritsail below her bowsprit; shortly
after she was launched spritsails were superseded by
triangular jibs. East Indiamen like this—bulky,
ponderous, dignified compromise craft with their air
of self-importance and their quasi-civilian/quasi-
military role—exemplified the companies themselves,
and carried the great bulk of the world's trade until
the middle of the nineteenth century.

An account, published in England in 1762, by an
unknown author gives a very clear picture of a
typical voyage to the East Indies and back. The
author arrived by coach at Gravesend to embark for
the Indies on Thursday, 30 July, 1746, and was
immediately plunged in drama. While watching the
arrival of the youths who had enlisted in the
company's service, he noted that: 'Among these came

a young person indifferently dressed, discovering a
very effeminate look and voice, and an awkward
carriage.' This young person was soon discovered to
be a woman when she had to present herself for a
medical inspection to 'the surgeon whose office it is
to examine all persons voyaging to be free from
infectious disease.' The poor girl proved to be
violently in love with a young man who had just
joined the ship in the service of the company.

Three days later they were off the Nore, at the
mouth of the Medway, and on 10 August they were in
Portsmouth, loading merchandise and treasure for
the voyage; the latter included a stone horse as a
present for the Sultan of Benjar, a kingdom in
Borneo. On 29 August they arrived in Cawsand Bay,
off Plymouth, where they were delayed by gales for
nearly three weeks. On 17 September, however, the
man-of-war *Mermaid* gave the signal for the convoy
to weigh anchor and the merchant fleet made sail to
the south and west.

Only a month later some of the passengers and
crew were showing signs of scurvy, for which fresh
water and exercise were prescribed. Some entertain-
ment was obviously had on board because when they
crossed the equator on 8 November all those for
whom this was a new experience had to subscribe a
bottle of brandy and a pound of sugar, or the sum of
two shillings and sixpence, towards the celebrations.
They also had trouble with the troops that were being
transported to Saint Helena since the writer says:
'We could hardly put a stop to the frequent thefts that
were committed by the soldiers, though every day one
or two of them were tied to the shrouds and severely
whipt.' On Christmas Eve, 1746, they sighted Saint

Helena, where they remained until 14 January, 1747.

Three months later they were round the Cape of Good Hope and close to the island of Saint Paul (midway between Africa and Australia), and on 19 April they dropped anchor in Batavia in the Dutch East Indies. They remained there for two months amid a minor political upheaval which, while it did not affect our author, did result in the imprisonment of the captain (one Congreve) and crew of another British East Indiaman. It also meant that the Sultan of Benjar did not get his horse.

They left Batavia for China on 11 June and took up a Chinese pilot off Macao at the entrance to the port of Canton on 8 July. When they moored alongside at Canton, they met one of the Dutch East Indiamen for the third time in the voyage, having first taken her for a pirate off Saint Helena and chased her till they discovered their mistake, and then rejoined her in Batavia. They stayed in Canton trading for four months and did not, in fact, leave until 11 January, 1748. At the beginning of March they were beset by gales but managed to wood and water at Price's Island; two days later they sighted some wreckage and picked up a Malayan seaman lost overboard from a Dutch East Indiaman off the coast of Madagascar. They later sighted the damaged merchantman with only her mizzen mast standing. She had jettisoned twenty-seven of the thirty guns she carried, and, our author notes: 'She rolled exceedingly with the swell.'

On 3 April, a year and four months after they had left, they re-anchored at Saint Helena, where they stayed three weeks repairing the storm damage and 'enjoying the benefits of genteel Female Society'. On the journey home in early summer everything went smoothly and a note for 1 June says: 'Employed almost every day exercising our guns and catching dolphins.' A more serious note is introduced on 25 June when: 'Not certain whether the war between Great Britain and France still continued we therefore proceeded with all possible speed to the North of Scotland.'

They anchored in Leith Roads in the afternoon of 9 July, 1748, having spent thirteen months and two weeks at sea and ten months in port. They were calculated to have sailed nine thousand leagues, or twenty-seven thousand miles. The only untypical thing about the voyage was that they were lucky enough never to have to fire their guns in anger either against the French or against pirates.

While John Company was trying his strength against his rivals in the Indian Ocean and the China Seas, all three nations were also endeavouring to locate the southern continent which, it was felt, must exist tidily to complete the world. This continent had been first postulated by Ptolemy but, due to the early establishment of a regular trade route across the Atlantic to Mexico and then across the northern part

of the Pacific to the Philippines and beyond, no one had bothered to sail south to seek it. When Quiros sailed from Spain with Luis de Torres in 1605, he was the first navigator to set out with the intention of discovering it—but he found the New Hebrides (which he called Australia de Espiritu Santo) instead. Torres remained in the Pacific and sailed north-west from their newly-discovered islands to circumnavigate New Guinea, but he hugged the southern shore of that island while going through the straits that now bear his name and so never sighted the sub-continent only a hundred miles or so south.

The Dutch East India Company sent Van Diemen to explore the South Pacific in 1642, and he added Tasmania, part of New Zealand, and the south coast of Australia to the growing map of the world. Bouvet discovered Cape Circumcision, not realizing that it was an island, for the French East India Company and claimed it as the tip of the southern continent. This caused a fair amount of confusion as later navigators—including Cook—were unable to re-discover it. Anson and Byron (in 1741 and 1764

The arrival of four ships of the Dutch
East India fleet at Amsterdam, 1599, by
Andries van Eertvelt. Much of the bustle
and prosperity of Amsterdam's golden age
of mercantile expansion is caught in this
evocative painting. National Maritime
Museum, Greenwich.

Below: An insurance agreement between a company of Madras insurers of Fort St George and Captain Parks. The ship *Morse* was insured for a voyage from Malacca to London via Canton for 5,000 star pagodas at a rate of seven pagodas per cent. Greater London Record Office.

Opposite: The lines of Captain Cook's *Endeavour*, 1768. The *Endeavour* really was 'a box with rounded corners'. Nevertheless she carried ninety-four men, their equipment and stores slowly but safely round the world. Science Museum, London.

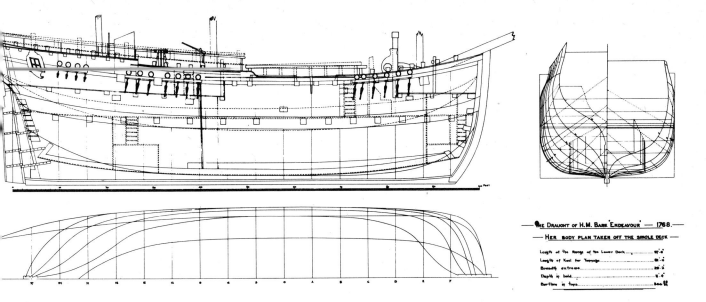

THE DRAUGHT OF H.M. BARK ENDEAVOUR — 1768. —
— HER BODY PLAN TAKEN OFF THE SINGLE DECK —

Length of the Range of the Lower Deck ....
Length of Keel for Tonnage ....
Breadth extreme ....
Depth in hold ....
Berthen in tons ....

respectively) sailed the Pacific without making any notable discoveries, but Wallis, who left shortly after Byron's return, discovered Tahiti – and called it George the Third's Island. Bouganville also visited Tahiti at almost the same time and he skirted the edge of the Great Barrier Reef on Australia's eastern seaboard but went no further. It was thus left to that incredibly painstaking and accurate self-made navigator Captain James Cook, R.N., F.R.S., to discover and explore the fertile east coast of Australia and claim it for the Crown. Cook proclaimed British sovereignty in 1770, but it was not until 1783 that it was suggested that this be supported, in fact, by the establishment of a convict settlement – an early form of assisted emigration. The first governor, Captain Phillip, a detachment of marines and 750 convicts landed in Botany Bay in January 1788. Six days later Lapérouse and a French squadron visited the bay on a voyage of exploration on behalf of the French Government but Lapérouse had regretfully to retire, remarking, 'In short, Mr Cook has done so much that he has left me nothing to do but to admire his work.'

The preparations for Cook's first voyage were extremely well worked out, perhaps because it was the Royal Society, supported by George III, who were the moving spirits. Astronomy was the main reason for the expedition: on 3 June, 1769, the planet Venus was due to transit the sun – a phenomenon which would not recur for more than a hundred years – and observation of this transit from different parts of the globe would give an accurate measurement of the distance of the earth from the sun. The king approved the project, and an expenditure of £4,000, and instructed the Admiralty to assist by providing a suitable vessel. However, a new ship had to be purchased for the voyage as no ship in the Service was thought wholly satisfactory. Probably at Cook's own insistence the choice fell on a Whitby collier brig – the *Earl of Pembroke*. She was renamed the *Endeavour* and became one of the most famous ships in the world.

The choice of one of these hardy little coasters is interesting, particularly if we remember Columbus's remarks about the *Santa Maria* being difficult to manoeuvre, too deep and generally unsuited for voyages of discovery. The *Endeavour* was only 368 tons, 100 feet long, 30 feet in beam and drew 13 feet

6 inches. She was thus small enough and shallow enough to poke her nose in almost anywhere. She was also roomy enough to accommodate a civilian complement of eight – Lieutenant Cook and Mr Green, observers; Mr Joseph Banks, naturalist, with his botanist companion, Dr Solander; Mr Sporing, another naturalist, and three artists, Mr Reynolds, Mr Parkinson and Mr Buchan – plus their scientific instruments and personal baggage, eighteen officers – two lieutenants, a surgeon, a master gunner, a boatswain, a carpenter, three master's mates, seven midshipmen, a clerk and a sergeant of marines – sixty-eight crew and enough stores for a voyage expected to last at least two years. All were neatly stowed into a volume about equal to that of two four-bedroomed semi-detached houses. The *Endeavour,* in common with her sister colliers, had a further advantage. She was built for working out of the harbours of the east coast with their winding river entrances and their complicated guardian shoals. Therefore, although not capable of any particular turn of speed, she was infinitely manoeuvrable: she could even sail backwards quite happily – a capability which Cook had to take advantage of when trapped in the Antarctic ice in the *Resolution* (another Whitby brig), on his second voyage.

There was another reason for Captain Cook's predilection for Whitby colliers – he learned his seamanship in them as ordinary seaman, able seaman and mate. In 1755, just as he was offered command of a coaster, he threw up this promising civilian career and joined the Navy as an able seaman. Within two years he had risen to the rank of master (the warrant officer who actually navigated the ship for the commissioned officers) and he was soon detached to survey the Saint Lawrence River and the coasts of Canada. The skill and accuracy that he demonstrated in the North Atlantic were the reasons for his promotion to lieutenant and his appointment as captain of the *Endeavour* to explore the South Pacific.

This remarkable man was not only an outstanding navigator; he showed the same painstaking care about the health and well-being of his crew as he did about the position and safety of his ship. During Anson's voyage he lost approximately a third of his men from sickness and injury before he was properly in the Pacific. Anson's chaplain, who wrote an

account of the voyage, noted that when they at last anchored off land and took the sick ashore they recovered wonderfully – he supposed that this was due to 'a subtle effluvium off the land' and thought that this explained why scurvy was relatively rare on land. Cook's approach was characteristically more scientific, and he took great interest in the 'anti-scorbutic principle' demonstrated by two doctors at Haslar Naval Hospital. The result of his insistence that his crew eat fresh meat and vegetables and, on his first voyage, a special malt for the prevention of scurvy, was an incredibly low incidence of sickness on board. At first the men objected to this, for them, unnatural sea diet and had to be flogged to eat fresh food; they also disliked the ventilation of the mess decks and the regular airing of their bedding but, by a combination of discipline and example, they changed at last from grudging acceptance to overwhelming enthusiasm for the new regimen.

An earlier and more disreputable voyage of note during the eighteenth century was that of George Shelvocke between 13 February, 1719, and 1 August, 1722, the immediate result of which was Shelvocke's (unsuccessful) prosecution for piracy. Shelvocke was born in 1675 and joined the Navy in about 1690, rising to lieutenant by 1704. This acting commission was confirmed by the Lord High Admiral in 1705. He transferred to the more profitable, though less "honourable", purser's branch in 1707, where he remained until 1713. He was "on the beach" for five years until his old shipmate Edward Hughes appointed him to lead a privateering expedition to the South Seas in November 1718.

The original idea was that the *Success* (350 tons, 36 guns) and the *Speedwell* (200 tons, 22 guns) should

have their names changed to *Prince Eugene* and *Staremberg* and sail under the flag of Charles VI, who was already at war with Spain. However problems, including Shelvocke's demotion to second-in-command, delayed the fitting out, and the ships finally sailed under their own names and with English letters of marque. The declaration made before the High Court of Admiralty shows that the 'owners and setters out' of the expedition were Edward Hughes, Henry Neale, Beake Winder and John Gumley. These gentlemen later formed a limited company whose share certificate read: 'This ticket entitles the Bearer to one share of Two Thousand Eight Hundred and Forty Shares, being equally divided, in the present Expedition of Captain John Clipperton, Commander in Chief of the Ships *Success* and *Speedwell,* fitted out and ordered to Cruise in the South Seas inder His Majesty's Commission and Letters of Mart issued from the Admiralty; and of all the Profits and Advantages arising by the Prizes or Captures already Taken or to be Taken by either of the said Ships, according to the agreements made by the Proprietors with the Commanders Officers and Ships Companys.'

The equipment of the *Speedwell,* according to the declaration made to the High Court, consisted of 22 guns, 100 small arms, 100 cutlasses, 25 barrels of powder, 20 rounds of 'great shot', 15 cwt of 'small shot', 2 suits of sails, 4 anchors, 4 cables and 15 cwt of spare cordage. The two ships left Bristol on 13 February, 1719, and six days later Shelvocke gave Clipperton the slip during a storm. Shelvocke's description of the storm, written in his *Apologia* published four years after his return to England, reads most alarmingly:

'By eleven of the clock we were under bare poles,

Opposite: The barque *Earl of Pembroke*
leaving Whitby harbour to be refitted for
Cook's voyage, 1768, attributed to Thomas
Luny (1759–1837). The *Earl of Pembroke*
was bought by the Admiralty for Cook's
first voyage–and renamed *Endeavour*.
National Library of Australia, Canberra.

Top: The departure of an English East
Indiaman, 1664, by Adam Willaerts. The
ordered bustle of departure is well captured
in this somewhat idealized seascape.
National Maritime Museum, Greenwich.

Bottom: East Indiamen off Deptford, 1721,
by Isaac Sailmaker. A particularly
interesting dockyard painting, showing
ships at various stages of construction.
National Maritime Museum, Greenwich.

Amsterdame Prospect von dem Ost-Indischen See-Magazin samt den großen Zimerplatz wo
die Kauffardey Schiffe gebauet, auch andere zu diesen Schiffen gehörige Sachen, gemacht und aufbehalten werden. Auf der Ostenburg am Ufer deß y, [ey] Flußes.

a, das große Magazin b, hier werden die Ancker u anders Eisenwerck geschmiedet c wo die Ochsen u anders zur Flotte
rige Sachen aufbehalten e, der Flachs boden wo das Schiff Seilwerck gemacht wird f hier wird das Schiff Thran geschmoltzen worin e

Vüe du Magazin des Indes Orientales à Amsterdam, avec le Chantier ou l'on construit les Vaisseaux pour les Indes, où l'on travaille aux Mâts, pouliers, rames, et à tout ce qui sert à la Navigation. Situé sur le bord du Ty, à l'endroit qu'on nome Oostenbourg.

...h, geschlachtet ü. eingesalzen wird. d. hier werden die großen Ancker Tau u. ü. Schiffs Seiler samt andern zu den Schiffen geho...
...ü. das Seilwerck eingedunckt ü. durchgezogen werden. Dieses Gebäude ist 2000. Schuch lang und 50 Schuch breit.

Delsenbach ad vivum fecit.

Previous page: The Dutch East India Company shipyard, Amsterdam, 1733, by J. A. Delsenbach. This view of an eighteenth-century shipyard underlines the sheer wealth of the great trading companies. Nederlandsch Historisch Scheepvaart Museum, Amsterdam.

Below: Ships trading in the East by Hendrik Cornelis Vroom (1566–1640). These Dutch East Indiamen are typical of the well-armed, well-found vessels of the period. National Maritime Museum, Greenwich.

with our yards a-portlast (i.e. lowered to the gunwales), not being able to suffer one knot of canvas all night, except, for a very little while, a reefed mizzen. About midnight a sea struck us upon the quarter, and drove in one of our quarter and one of our stern dead lights, where we shipped great quantities of water, before we were able to stop them up again, and were for a considerable time under continued apprehensions of foundering. This accident exposed us to the greatest danger. We were not able to get the ship before the wind, nor could we work the pumps upon deck, the lee pump being all the time under water; and besides this, had a succession of prodigious seas driving over us, so that none could stand on their legs.'

The crew were all for turning smartly about and going back to England. Shelvocke therefore mustered them on deck and explained that the *Speedwell* was really quite a handy ship and it was only the vast quantity of stores they had on board that made her tender; he told them that they 'should, in a little time, eat and drink her into a better trim' and followed up the promise by ordering a double tot of brandy all round.

Shelvocke and Clipperton did not rendezvous at the Cape Verde Islands as appointed–though each states that he awaited the other. The *Success* departed for the Pacific on 2 April; Shelvocke and the *Speedwell* did not leave the Cape Verdes until 20 April. He then sailed towards the coast of Brazil, where he persuaded a merchantman to provide "presents" of China silk, cups and plates and 300 moidores. With the silk he had his officers decorate their red and gold suits in a most smart and attractive manner. Shelvocke himself favoured black *peau-de-soie* with silver frogging across the chest.

Although his voyage had hardly started and they were still in the Atlantic, he was continually having trouble with his crew. On 31 July his nine officers, all the petty officers and thirty-six hands demanded agreement to a list of articles for the division of plunder because 'We have very good reason to believe that if we shall have the fortune to make this voyage should be carried to London, we should never receive half thereof; for it is known to all, how the people on board the ships *Duke* and *Dutchess* were treated.' The Articles read:

'Imprimis, That our part of each prize we take shall be equally divided, as soon as possible, after the capture thereof, between the ship's company, according to each man's respective shares, as borne on the ship's books.

'Secondly, That all plunder on board each prize we take shall be equally divided among the ship's company, according to each man's respective shares, as above.

'Thirdly, That gold rings found in any place, except in a goldsmith's shop, is plunder; all arms,

sea-books and instruments, all clothing and moveables usually worn about prisoners (except women's ear-rings, unwrought gold and silver, loose diamonds, pearls and money), all plate in use aboard ships, but not on shore (unless about the persons of prisoners) is plunder; all manner of clothes ready-made, found on the upper deck, or between decks, belonging to the ship's company or passengers, is plunder also, except what is above limited, and is in bundles of pieces not opened in the country, that appears not for the person's use that owns the chest, but designed for merchandize, which only shall not be plunder; all manner of bedding, all manner of necessaries, all buttons, buckles, liquors and provisions, for our own expending and use, is plunder. It is also agreed that any sort of wrought silver and gold, crucifixes, gold and silver watches, or any other moveables found about the prisoners, or any wearing apparel of any kind, shall likewise be plunder.

'Fourthly, That if any person on board the ship do conceal any plunder, exceeding one piece of eight, twenty-four hours after the capture of the prize, he shall be severely punished, and lose his share of that prize and plunder one half thereof to be given to the informer, and the other to be equally divided among the ship's company. The same penalty to be inflicted for being drunk in time of action, or disobeying his superior officer's command, or concealing himself in the sea or land service, except when any prize is taken by storm or boarding. Then whatsoever is taken shall be his own, as follows, *viz.* a sailor or landman 10 *l*, a mate, gunner, boatswain and carpenter 40 *l*, a lieutenant or master 80 *l*, and the captain 100 *l*.

'Fifthly, That all plunder shall be appraised and divided as soon as possible after the capture; also every person to be sworn and searched, as soon as they come aboard, by such persons as shall be appointed for that purpose. The person or persons refusing, shall forfeit their share of the prize or plunder as above.

'Sixthly, In consideration that Captain Shelvocke, to make the ship's company easy, has given the whole cabin plunder (which, in all probability, is the major part) to be divided as aforesaid, we do voluntarily agree, that he shall have five *per cent* over and above his respective share, as a consideration of what is his due of the plunder aforesaid.

'Seventhly, That a reward of twenty dollars shall be given to him that first sees a prize of good value, or exceeding fifty tons in burthen.'

All of which goes to show that, while there may be honour, there is not much trust among privateers.

They had quite a successful cruise up the western coast of South America, taking various prizes, but were shipwrecked on the island of Juan Fernandez—according to some, Captain Shelvocke engineered it. The only provisions they salvaged were one cask of beef and one of *farina de Pao* but Shelvocke fortunately saved eleven hundred dollars 'which were kept in my chest in the great cabin'. Mutiny yet again raised its head, with the ship's cobbler as spokesman, but the men were so divided amongst themselves that Shelvocke was able to continue to command, albeit precariously. The first thing they did was to set about building a boat, from which they fished and also attempted to salvage some of the wreck of the *Speedwell*; they also started to build a 'bark' of twenty tons burthen. She was launched on 5 October, five months after their shipwreck, and named the *Recovery*.

Within a month they had captured a Spanish ship of some two hundred tons, the *Jesus Maria,* soon

Ship Dutton from London towards Madras

H	K	F	Courses	Winds	Monday the 4 July 1791
1	4	4	E S°	N E°	Mod° & Pleasant Weat'
2	4	2			People emp'd by the
3	4	6			Boatswain and the
4	4	2			Tradesmen in their
5	4	6		N b N	necessary duty.
6	5	2			Var'd p'
7	5	4			Azm° 25.12 9 W'
8	5	3			Ham'd 25.25 }
9	5	2			
10	5	4			
11	5	2			
12	4	4			
1	4	"		N b W'	
2	4	"			
3	3	2		N W°	Cloudy.
4	2	6			
5	3	"			Bar' Ham'd 26.00 W'
6	3	2			Find by our Time keepers we have had a set to the E'wd
7	4	"			of 44 miles —
8	4	"			
9	4	2		North	Hazy a little past Noon fell
10	5	"			from the Main Top G'yard Alex'
11	6	3			Carson 1 of B'rs' the Ship too
12	6	"			immediately, and flung over board

Lat° Ob'd 37.51 S'

a spar, but before the boat could
be lowered down, altho' every possible
exertion was made of he disappeared
'Tis apprehended as he fell on the Main
sheet block & from thence over board
that he had been killed, or so much
hurt as to be unable to keep himself above water. Bore away & made
Sail.

Var° GD 67
2 W 64

110

Course	Dist'	N	S°	M D	Lat' Ob'd	x Long	Long'd in	Long'd by T. Keepers
N° 81 E°	110	17	110	26 51 E° 37.52	2.19 25 39		N° 25 — 25 37 9 E'
								237 — 26 42 }
								354 — 27 30 }

Dutch East Indiamen near the shore, 1693, by William van der Velde the Elder. This grisaille dramatically illustrates the strength of the East Indiamen's construction and firepower. National Maritime Museum, Greenwich.

renamed the *Happy Return*. In her, during the following January, they fell in several times with Captain Clipperton in the *Success,* who, curiously, did not receive his former subordinate with open arms. However, some time later the two came together with the intention of capturing the Manila ship. (This ship transported the silver treasure of the Philippines to Spain and was the richest prize on the high seas.) But now it was the turn of Clipperton to give his consort the slip, and this upset the honest Shelvocke no end: 'Thus we cruised in good order, and with a great deal of hope, until March 17, the time appointed for me to suffer the most cruel and perfidious piece of treachery that could be committed.'

During March 1721 Shelvocke captured another Spanish ship, the *Sacra Familia,* which they had to exchange for the *Happy Return* in order to escape from Dom Manuel de Medino Solerzaro, Governor of Sonsonnate, or la Trinidad, on the western coast of Mexico. The spiteful Spaniard wanted to have them all hanged for piracy in spite of Shelvocke's protests that 'I will never act any thing contrary to the orders of my Sovereign Lord, his Britannic Majesty.' They continued their voyage until they arrived in Canton, where Shelvocke sold his ship for 2,000 taels and took passage home in an East India Company's ship—the *Cadogan.*

Although poor Shelvocke was so monstrously put upon and his share of the profits of the trading venture so greatly reduced—'I must here observe that every thing we took was divided according to the Juan Fernandian articles, and I had no more than six instead of sixty shares.'—he did not really do badly. His share of the booty from one silver transport alone was £2,642 10s., and his profit from the whole voyage over £7,000—at today's values probably something like a quarter of a million pounds sterling. I think that this commercial success entitles the voyage to be included among "merchant adventures", although its character was wholly warlike or piratical.

The commercial monopoly in the East Indies and the necessity for dual-purpose ships, fit for trade and war, meant that there was no incentive for improvement of design. The West Indian trade, however, was not a monopoly and so there was competition between the carriers and a development of the ships engaging in that trade. The main differences were that, without sacrificing any sea-keeping qualities, the West Indiamen had a greater cargo capacity and required about half the crew of an East Indiaman of similar tonnage. The main similarity between European merchantmen towards the end of the eighteenth century was that they were all relatively beamy for their length: the proportion being normally four to one. Also, since they were built for long-distance ocean cruising, they were all square-rigged—still the best rig for running down the trade winds.

The Barque *Caesar,* hove-to off Georgetown, Demerara, 1839. An indication of the finer lines and flared bow of a West Indiaman. The handsome schooner (*left*) may be engaged in the slave trade. National Maritime Museum, Greenwich.

Chapter five
The development of the American marine

Ships have been essential to the North American settlers ever since they were used for the exploration of the continent. The original settlements were naturally on the seaboard and the best method of penetrating inland was by water, up the rivers and across lakes the size of seas. Before the railroads opened up the interior, communication between the centres on the eastern coast was fastest, most convenient, and economical by ship. However, colonial shipbuilding was of little historical importance since firstly no one thought of encouraging the emigration of shipwrights so little building took place, and secondly, what ships were built were on a European model. But after the passing of the 1651 Navigation Act—which ended the Dutch supremacy in coastal and overseas shipping—boat-building started to flourish. The names of the early sites are part of the fabric of American history: Mystic, Merrimac, Charles and Connecticut; Salem, Scituate, Beverly and Boston.

There are as many myths about American ship-building as there are about the Wild West—and, as with the legends of cowboys and Indians, Wells-Fargo and the Pony Express, there is a certain amount of historical fact behind the fiction. But of one thing there can be no doubt, the newly independent Americans very rapidly adopted the schooner as their national rig. The 'schooner' was no more an American invention than the tin can or the motor car but it met their requirements of speed and economy and they developed it with skill and affection. Even their enemies admitted this. Howard Chapelle quotes William James as saying: 'None can compete with the Americans in the size, beauty, swiftness or seaworthiness of their schooners.' This is praise indeed because James was a lifelong opponent of the Americans after being interned in America at the beginning of the War of 1812. In fact, from then onwards he devoted himself to writing books and pamphlets on the English and American navies to counteract the American claims to superior skill and courage at sea. While overall his *Account of the Naval War* is biased, it is extremely interesting because James did not merely compare the conflicting official reports but interviewed many of the officers and men on both sides.

The main virtues of the schooner are ease of handling—fore-and-aft rigs are easier to hoist, reef

and stow than square sails, without the need to go aloft—weatherliness, or the ability to make to windward, and speed on a beam wind. Speed not only suited the American character, it was a necessity for survival for many years. The eastern seaboard and the Caribbean—with whom the young colony had a flourishing trade—were the haunt of pirates and freebooters before the Declaration of Independence and later they were blockaded by the British during the War of American Independence and the War of 1812. There were two other less reputable reasons for the emphasis on speed. One was the slave trade, for which fast vessels were essential: firstly to try to preserve the perishable cargo, and secondly to evade British warships after the Abolition in 1815. The other was to evade the Preventative Men while engaged in the profitable business of smuggling with the West Indies. Competition between smugglers and revenue men has always been good for the boat-building trade, often resulting in a yard with a reputation for slippery ships building a revenue cutter and, say, a smuggling schooner on adjoining slipways.

So, while the British, French and Dutch were building deep, full-bodied, ponderous and powerful square-rigged East Indiamen protected from competition by their monopolies, the Americans were developing a leaner type of craft with a fine entry and more rise to her floor. These ships had less cargo space but were faster and needed smaller crews than the European square-riggers; their rapid turn-round and economical running costs made them highly profitable and it was estimated that nine-tenths of the American foreign trade in 1814 was being carried in the swift and elegant Baltimore clippers. Here we come again to the problem of the names of ships—'clipper' does not really describe any particular type of ship but simply means a fast one that "clips along" The name should really be reserved, perhaps, for the cranky, over-extended ships built in America for the California passenger trade when the gold fever whipped up the passion for speed to uneconomic levels, but the later development of more seaworthy ships for the China and Australia trade produced those beautiful ships that are now most commonly called clippers.

American schooners did not only carry goods between the eastern states, Europe and the West Indies. There was a flourishing trade in grain, coal

Top: The shipyard on Gray's Inn Creek, Kent County, Maryland, an unsigned painting formerly over the fireplace of Spencer Hall in Talbot County. This pre-revolutionary painting shows a great variety of colonial shipping, including brigs, sloops and small bay craft. Maryland Historical Society, Baltimore, Maryland.

Bottom: A view of New Amsterdam, 1651, by Hartger. Ships played an important part in the establishment and extension of colonial America. Prints Division, The New York Public Library, Astor, Lenox and Tilden Foundations, New York.

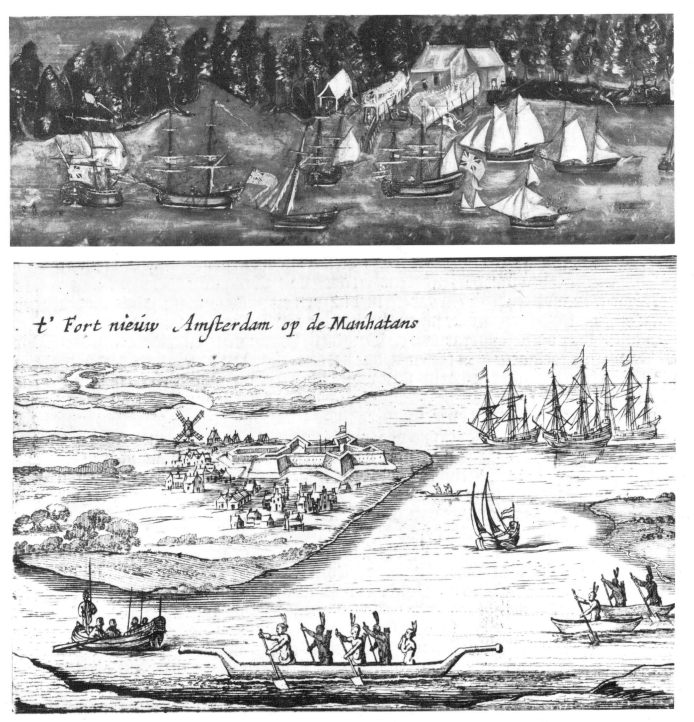

t' Fort nieúw Amsterdam op de Manhatans

and ore carried in two-, three- and four-masted schooners on the Great Lakes, that fantastic chain of sizeable seas a thousand miles inland. Schooners also fished the Grand Banks and raced each other to port with all the skill and enthusiasm that captured and retained the *America*'s Cup (won by a schooner against all comers, although under slightly peculiar circumstances). In fact this fore-and-aft rig, with more and more masts added as ships grew longer, was providing economic power for sailing ships right up to the start of the Second World War. Though, while the *Thomas Lawson,* a seven-masted schooner nearly four hundred feet long and displacing over five thousand tons, fits the 'size' part of William James's description of American schooners, I am not sure that she merits the word 'beauty'. This enormous sailing vessel, built in 1902, was managed by a crew of only sixteen. She was finally lost on the Scilly Islands in December 1907 carrying a cargo of oil – a forgotten fore-runner of the *Torrey Canyon.*

For three thousand years merchant ships had been distinguished from warships by an adjective: "long" ships were warships and "round" ships were merchantmen. All true merchantmen from the Egyptians up to the middle of the eighteenth century were built with bluff, round bows and an almost square cross-section. In America this began gradually to change, starting with the Baltimore clipper schooners. As more speed was demanded so the hull became longer in proportion to its breadth, the lines of the bow became hollow and the ship's bottom

became more vee-shaped. When the California gold rush was at its height the demand for swift transport was paramount and owners built longer, narrower, leaner and more canvassed ships chasing this profitable trade. They soon over-extended themselves as much as they had over-extended their ships because these 'clippers' were weak in construction, cranky to sail and demanded too much of their uneconomically large crew. However, due to their great length and hard driving they did make some very fast passages, and while the boom in California lasted they also made their owners money. There have been more theories as to which was the first clipper ship than there are varieties of canned food by a well-known manufacturer – and all to no point, because, by the nature of ship design, there was no exact time when one could say 'This is an ordinary packet and that is a clipper'. The *Rainbow* has often been given the credit for being the first, but, although she was a very handsome boat with a very fast hull, she was not of an original shape when compared with the earlier *Hannibal* or the privateer *Rattlesnake.*

With the repeal of the Navigation Acts in 1849, trade between England and the rest of the world was thrown open and the American clippers began to compete with – or rather at first overwhelm – the British carriers of tea from China. These magnificent "Down Easters" could make so handsome a profit on the passage from the Atlantic coast to San Francisco as to allow them to sail in ballast to China and then compete with British ships in the trade to England.

The *Oriental,* in 1850, made the passage from Hong Kong in a record ninety-seven days, and in 1852 the *Witch of the Wave* sailed from Canton to the Deal Roads in only ninety days.

These early clippers were magnificent to see but hell to sail and their skippers and crews were rough, tough and often unmanageable. But there was another hazard for even the more humane ships' officers, the power of the Press. The racing clippers of the 1850s were the pop stars of their time. Their vital statistics were publicized and discussed, their last performances compared with their competitors' and the characters of their captains dissected and sometimes destroyed by the sensation-seeking papers. One famous ship-master who was almost destroyed in this way was Captain Waterman, who had made his name in the *Sea Witch* on the China run. In 1848 the Griswold brothers' 2000-ton ship the *Challenge* was launched from William Webb's New York yard. She sailed for San Francisco with fifty-six men on board under the command of Captain Waterman and was dogged by bad luck from the very start. She was, after all, a brand-new ship which had not yet shaken down and seems to have had a particularly dissolute and dangerous crew. After a voyage of 108 days they arrived in San Francisco with four men dead from injuries and five dead from sickness. The crew then deserted and, to cover themselves, visited the offices of the 'California Courier'. The editor swallowed their story and produced the following dramatic editorial:

'The ship *Challenge* has arrived here, and Captain Waterman, her commander, has also, **but where are nine men of his crew?** Where is Waterman and his guilty First Mate Douglas? The sworn testimony given against them by members of the crew, if really true, makes them the most inhuman monsters of this age. If these accounts be proven correct, then Waterman at least ought to be burned alive. Nine of his crew are missing, and the survivors who are with us declare that four were shaken from the ship's mizen topsail yard into the sea off Cape Horn, where they were left to drown, and five other men died from the results of wounds and ill-treatment.

'Five of the survivors who came ashore yesterday were mangled and bruised in the most shocking manner; one poor fellow died early today and four others, it is expected, will very soon be in the cold embrace of death.

'We can only trust that all humane men will turn out and pursue Waterman until his arrest and punishment.'

This leader was so successful that a mob of some two thousand 'humane men' turned out and, not finding the captain, burned the offices of the owners, Griswold, to the ground. In order to protect himself and to clear his name Waterman stood trial at his own request. The trial exposed the allegations for the criminal fiction that they were and the 'Courier' came out with the following near apology:

'We are now informed that a state of feeling exists between a few of the seamen who made the voyage from New York (in the *Challenge*) . . . but this is

widely different from that which we reported ... Nine members of the crew have ... expressed their willingness to make the outward passage to Canton in the ship, under Captain Waterman. They have made sworn statements proving that the course Captain Waterman pursued from New York Harbour to San Francisco Bay anchorage was fully justified.'

Waterman, however, had had enough of hardship at sea leading to slander on land and very shortly retired, a respected citizen, to a house he built on the outskirts of San Francisco.

Apart from the development of the schooner in all its forms and the 'invention' of the long, slim clipper shape for fast carriers and packets, the other great American interest was in whaling. Over three hundred whaling ships were sailing out of New Bedford alone in the middle 1850s. A great number of these 'whale-ships' were converted packet-ships but as the trade increased so more ships were built specially for it. When seen afloat these ship-rigged craft were easily recognizable by the whale-boats slung in davits along their sides. Underwater they were also differentiated from other ships, by the sharp rise to their floor and easy turn to their bilges. This helped their sailing qualities in the difficult seas in which they had to operate but their lines were really so drawn to allow them to heel over easily when 'cutting-out' a whale.

Slavery is bound up with American history, or rather, with the whole history of the Americas and the Caribbean. I have already touched on the fact

that, like all branches of commerce with special requirements, the slave trade had an influence on ship design. The ships needed to be shallow to navigate the estuaries on the African coast, they needed to be fast to preserve their perishable cargo and they also needed to be weatherly to avoid capture by the naval ships implementing the abolition of slavery after 1815. The Government was officially opposed to the traffic but the strong Southern lobby effectively drew its teeth, and in the 1830s Havana was the clearing house for the American slave trade. The trade was extremely profitable: a healthy male would fetch about $450 in Havana, and the coastal traders who ran slaves up to Florida, Georgia and Carolina would ask at least $1,000 apiece. A small coaster carrying some fifty slaves would gross $25,000 or £6,000 each trip.

Until the beginning of the nineteenth century, slavery was regarded as a fact of life and slave trading was both respectable and essential (or thought to be) to national prosperity. John Newton, a British slave ship's captain, the son of a shipmaster, wrote in his diary in 1753 that 'He thanked God that he had been led into an easy and creditable way of life.' Three years later he had changed his opinions and wrote, 'Thus I was brought out of a way of life, disagreeable to my temper and inconvenient to my profession.' Newton later entered the Church; he was ordained in 1764 and appointed curate at Olney where, with Cowper, he wrote the Olney Hymns. Years after, he was in a position to influence William

Top: The launch of the *Glory of the Seas* from Donald McKay's shipyard at East Boston, 1869. He built the *Lightning* which logged 436 miles in 24 hours in 1856. Peabody Museum, Salem, Massachusetts.

Bottom: The 2454-ton *John B. Prescott,* the largest five-masted schooner ever built. It was launched in 1898, together with the 2440-ton *Nathaniel T. Palmer.* They were designed to compete for the bulk cargo trade with steamships, but of course they failed. Peabody Museum, Salem, Massachusetts.

Wilberforce to join the Abolitionists. Newton left a journal of three voyages between 1750 and 1754, which is probably the only remaining record of slaving as seen by a slave ship's captain.

His first ship was the *Duke of Argyle,* a snow. The distinctive points of a snow were that it was a smallish two-masted vessel, square-rigged on both masts, with the addition of a gaff sail set on a subsidiary mast just behind the mainmast. This meant that she was able to choose between setting a square or a fore-and-aft mainsail, the first for running down the trades and the latter for clawing to windward and manoeuvring in confined spaces.

Newton's first voyage started on 11 August, 1750, when he left Liverpool and ran down to the mouth of the river to wait for a fair wind. The next ten days illustrate the disadvantages of having to rely on the wind as he was forced to lie at anchor employing the hands on any odd jobs that could be found: 'Fixed the new trysail . . . People at work making sinnet, swabs etc. . . . Carpenter mended the channel bend, and fixed the backstay plate . . .' However, at noon on 20 August they weighed anchor and were 'working with a small brease at North'. A month later they

were off the Canaries and Newton was pleased to observe that 'My octant agrees very well with the latitude laid down in the *Mariner's Compass* . . . I am consequently not less than 50 leagues to the Eastward of my reckoning which . . . must be owing to a strong current setting to the Eastward, which cannot suppose less than 20 miles *per diem.*' At the beginning of October, surrounded by flying fish and turtles, the carpenter was set to work preparing the ship to receive her unfortunate cargo. On 19 October Newton was able to enter in his journal, 'Saw the land, Sierra Leon, bearing SE 16 leagues, and the largest island of the Idolo's NE b.E 7 leagues . . . I find that I was too hasty in condemning my reckoning, for it has answered to a great exactness.'

Newton spent about a month repairing and renewing the ship's boats and missing the purchase of slaves by one accident or another: 'I was unluckily deprived of a boat [by the crew being drunk] when I wanted to go on board to see Ord's slaves, by which means Ellis got 5, being all there were worth chusing . . . brought a woman slave whom I refused being long breasted . . . Believe I have lost the purchase of more than 10 slaves for want of the all

...representation of the brig Vigilante from Nantes, a vessel employed in the Slave Trade, which was captured by Lieutenant ...dmay, in the River Bonny, on the Coast of Africa, on the 15th of April 1822. She was 240 Tons burden & had on ...d, at the time she was taken 345 Slaves. The Slaves were found lying on their backs on the lower deck, as represented ... these in the centre were sitting, some in the posture in which they are there shewn & others with their legs bent under ... resting upon the soles of their feet.

Fig. 1.
Longitudinal Section of the Ship

Length of the lower deck at AA 81 F.t 7 I.s
Height between decks from deck to deck 4 F.t 8 I.s

Water Line

Fig. 2.
Plan of the upper deck

Length of the upper deck at II 92 Feet
Breadth   D.o   KK 27 F.t 3 I.s

Sky light   Ladder way Captains Cabin   Gro   ti   Ro.   Pump   Main Hatch   Fore Hatch   Place for Women   Place for Slaves   Seamens Fire Place

Fig. 6.

Fig. 7.

Fig. 8.

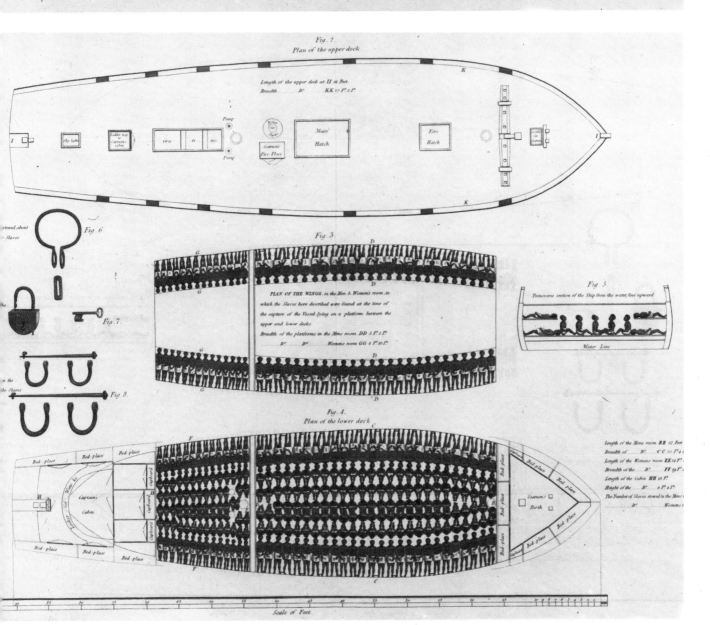

Fig. 3.

PLAN OF THE WINGS, in the Men's & Women's room, in which the Slaves here described were found at the time of the capture of the Vessel, lying on a platform between the upper and lower decks.
Breadth of the platforms in the Mens room DD 5 F.t 3 I.s
    D.o   D.o   Womens room GG 4 F.t 10 I.s

Fig. 5.
Transverse section of the Ship from the water line upward

Water Line

Fig. 4.
Plan of the lower deck

Bed place   Captains Cabin   Seamens Birth   Bed place

Length of the Mens room BB 32 Feet
Breadth of   D.o   CC 22 F.t 4 I.s
Length of the Womens room EE 14 F.t
Breadth of the   D.o   FF 19 F.t
Length of the Cabin HH 10 F.t
Height of the   D.o   6 F.t 4 I.s
The Number of Slaves stowed in the Mens r.
    D.o   Womens r.

Scale of Feet.

75

commanding articles of beer and cyder . . .' However, business picked up on 12 November when he bought his first four slaves–three men and a woman. By the beginning of December he had twenty-six slaves on board and a ton and a half of camwood (*kambi,* the African red hard wood, used for dyes and in violin bows). January saw them 150 miles further south down the coast with forty-three slaves aboard; by this time dysentery and fever were beginning to attack his crew and two had already died.

He continued to cruise down the coast with the ship's boats exploring ahead of him, seeking out trade, but he had still not completed his cargo in mid-May and was not hopeful as to his prospects, 'In the forenoon hove up the anchor to look at; being clear, let it go again. Bought a man and a girl (4 feet 1 inch) from a quiet fellow who called himself Jemmy, which took away my last kettle, except one broke, and the remainder of my beads, so that I believe my trade for this voyage is finished. However, shall wait here till morning because the man that was on board yesterday promised to sell me two more for arms and powder.' On 22 May, with 174 slaves on board, he wrote, 'At 3 a.m. weighed with a small brease at West, bound (by God's permission) for Antigua.' For the next few days he was occupied with problems of navigation: 'I am obliged to estimate the longitude myself for it is not laid down in the books, and those places that are, very incorrectly.' Fortunately for Captain Newton he was not wholly preoccupied because on 26 May he had to write, 'In the evening, by the favour of Providence, discovered a conspiracy among the men slaves to rise upon us, but a few hours before it was to have been executed. A young man who has been the whole voyage out of irons, first on account of a large ulcer, and since for his seeming good behaviour, gave them a large marline spike down the gratings, but was happily seen by one of our people. They had it in their possession about 1 hour before I made search for it, in which time they made such good dispatch (being an instrument that made no noise) that this morning I've found near 20 of them had broke their irons.'

For the next fortnight the weather remained cold and cloudy although they were in the heart of the tropics and this caused further problems for the captain: 'Got the slaves up this morn. Washed them all with fresh water. They complained so much of the cold that was obliged to let them go down again when the room was cleared . . . can hardly keep them warm in the rooms . . . Am obliged to keep the slaves close down, and even the tarpaulins laid over.' But, on 3 July: 'Were abreast of the breakers at 9 a.m. and soon after saw Antigua; bore away for it . . .' Newton traded his slaves, loaded with sugar, and sailed for Liverpool on 13 August, where they arrived on 7 October. One entry that brings out the problems of early navigation is that for 1 October: 'At 1 p.m. bore down and spoke to the brig, being of and for Bristol from Newfoundland only 12 days out. The master reckoned himself 75 leagues to the Westward of Cape Clear . . . by my reckoning I am, at noon, 19 leagues to the Westward of Cape Clear.' The next day's entry reads, 'As I have overrun my difference in longitude I must depend on a good look out instead of a bad reckoning.' John Newton was sailing ten years before Harrison perfected his Chronometer Number Four.

He makes no entry as to the profitability of his voyage or indeed of his later voyages, but he does say in his *Authentic Narrative,* 'I was upon the whole satisfied with it [the slave trade], as the appointment Providence had worked out for me; yet it was, in many respects, far from eligible. It is, indeed, accounted a genteel employment and is usually very profitable, though to me it did not prove so, the Lord seeing that a large increase in wealth would not be good for me.' Of his ship's complement of thirty crew and 174 slaves on the 1750 voyage he lost seven crew members and twenty-eight slaves. That this was almost certainly due to the execrably overcrowded conditions found on board a slaver is borne out by the unique voyage of 1753 when Newton was unable to fill his cargo space and sailed with only eighty-seven slaves. He lost neither a slave nor a crewman: 'This was much noticed, and spoken of in the town; and I believe it is the first instance of its kind.'

Opposite: Multi-masted schooners at Newport News, Virginia, in 1906. The seven-masted vessel is the *Thomas W. Lawson*: 5,000 tons and handled by a crew of sixteen men. The others (three masts upwards) are *Sallie I'on, Malcolm Baxter Jr, Jennie French* and *Eleanor A. Percy*. Mariners Museum, Newport News, Virginia.

Below: Sailing ships lying alongside the South Street piers, New York City, *circa* 1890. Staten Island Historical Society, Richmondtown, Staten Island, New York.

Chapter six
The full flowering of ocean sailing

In May 1812 the British Prime Minister, Spencer Perceval, was assassinated; he was succeeded by Robert Jenkinson, Earl of Liverpool, who brought into his administration Robert Peel, George Canning and, as President of the Board of Trade, William Huskisson. Each one of these men had a far-reaching effect on Britain's future. Canning's doctrine of non-interference and Peel's police are well known. Huskisson was a free trader and repealed the Navigation Acts in 1849. They were deleted from the statute book at about the same time as the duty on iron and cotton was lowered by 70 per cent and the duty on both the import and export of wool cut by nearly as much. This had a profound effect on the world's shipping trade and, contrary to the British merchants' prophecies of doom, led to an increase of nearly 50 per cent in the tonnage of the British mercantile marine in the next twenty years. The system of measurement of ships for registration was also altered at about this time, making it practicable to build longer, slimmer, faster ships than before.

Two other, unrelated, factors exerted their influence on ship design in the middle of the nineteenth century. Gold was discovered in California in 1847, and steam tugs became both efficient and reliable. The latter meant, of course, that sailing ships had no longer to be capable of manoeuvring into port under sail.

After the War of 1812, the European emigrant packet trade gradually increased. This led, of course, to an increase in the number of ships employed in that trade. The high-profit freight and the relatively short distance of the crossing – and also the passengers' preference – put a premium on speed and rapid turn-round. This led to a gradual sharpening of ship lines and an increase in the sail area. The Americans, with their lack of restrictions on measured tonnage, started this trend from the yards of Brown and Bell, Isaac Webb, Smith and Dimon, Henry Eckford and Donald McKay. However, steamers had started on the Atlantic run by the 1840s, and sailing ships became unprofitable by the early '50s, although they could hold their own on longer passages.

The next demand for rapid transport was the California gold rush which, as mentioned in the previous chapter, produced the really extreme clippers. The *Rainbow, Young America, Lightning* and

The first-class packet ship *Yorkshire* of
New York, 1840. The *Yorkshire* was one
of the famous Black Ball Line packets
plying between Liverpool and New York.
National Maritime Museum, Greenwich.

the *Herald of the Morning* and many others became household words in an over-publicized and over-romantic age. The *Lightning,* which was built by Donald McKay for James Baines's Black Ball Line Liverpool-to-Australia packets in 1853, had a registered tonnage of 1,468; she was 244 feet long, 44 feet broad and 23 feet deep. Her main saloon was 86 feet long and she had the luxury of 8 feet of headroom between decks. She was designed to set 13,000 square yards of canvas on three masts–the main 164 feet tall, the foremast 151 feet and the mizzen 115 feet tall–and she cost £32,000 fitted out. On her delivery voyage she sailed from Boston to Liverpool in just under fourteen days. On her maiden voyage to Melbourne under 'Bully' Forbes and 'Bully' Bragg as captain and first mate she made the passage, in spite of light weather, in seventy-seven days. Twice during the voyage the *Lightning* ran for twenty-four hours at an average of eighteen knots–logging 436 and 430 sea miles respectively–and between 28 June and 4 July, 1856, she logged 2,188 miles across the southern Indian Ocean.

Life on board a packet ship was not always pleasant for the passengers, as this extract from an account by Captain Paddy Ryan of the *Margaret* shows:

'Two days out of our home port we encountered the makings of a full gale and the ship was caught abeam by a heavy sea, she all but capsized, with my crew managing to save themselves by hanging on for dear life to anything that promised, however remotely, to stay firm, while, above our heads, the sails bellied and cracked and were finally ripped to shreds and our topmasts bent like willows while the mizzen topsail was wrenched clean from its bolts and carried out of sight downwind. The storm passed as quickly as it came up and the crew set-to and cleaned up and the ship was put on a fresh tack, but the weather deteriorated and a fresh gale struck, with alarming effect, the ship rearing up until it seemed she might assume the perpendicular. When at last we ran clear of bad weather we made new sail, refitted the stateroom galley and my passengers sat down to their first hot meal in five days. Throughout the spell of inclement conditions I was forced to keep my three hundred and seventy-five steerage passengers, men, women and children, under hatches. Many of them exhausted their food supplies before the ship made port and I felt great pity for the poor souls. The weather easing, I ordered hatches to be raised, and as they were opened clouds of steam arose on the cold air, and the resulting stench might well have come from a farm pig-stye, and gave me sickness in my hardened stomach. Before the ship made port five babies were born among the emigrants, their mothers attended in labour by the carpenter, a resourceful man, whose duties included the pulling of teeth among the ailing emigrants. Two male Irish passengers from the

Top: The British East India Company's experimental iron ships, 1840. The brig *Guide* is to the left and the barque *John Laird* to the right. National Maritime Museum, Greenwich.

Bottom: A constructional model of a merchant ship, *circa* 1845. Accurate models like this were built to show prospective buyers exactly what they would get for their money. Science Museum, London.

Next page: The 1608-ton clipper *Hurricane,* built by Isaac C. Smith, Hoboken, New Jersey. This elegant ship portrait demonstrates the grace and power of the later clippers. Peabody Museum, Salem, Massachusetts.

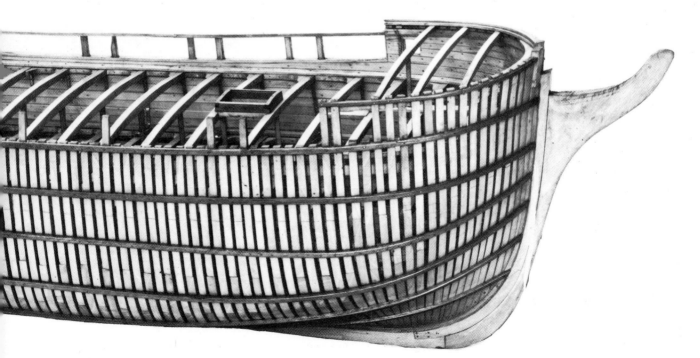

Top: A drawing of the hull of a composite (wood and iron) ship, 1866. The almost photographic drawing shows the diamond-shaped lattice which provided resistance to hogging with the least weight. Science Museum, London.

Bottom: An indenture of apprenticeship, dated 1831. William Collins, who was bound apprentice in the Southern Whale Fishery ship *Seringapatam*, was tragically killed only thirty-four months later, falling from the foretopsail yard. Greater London Record Office.

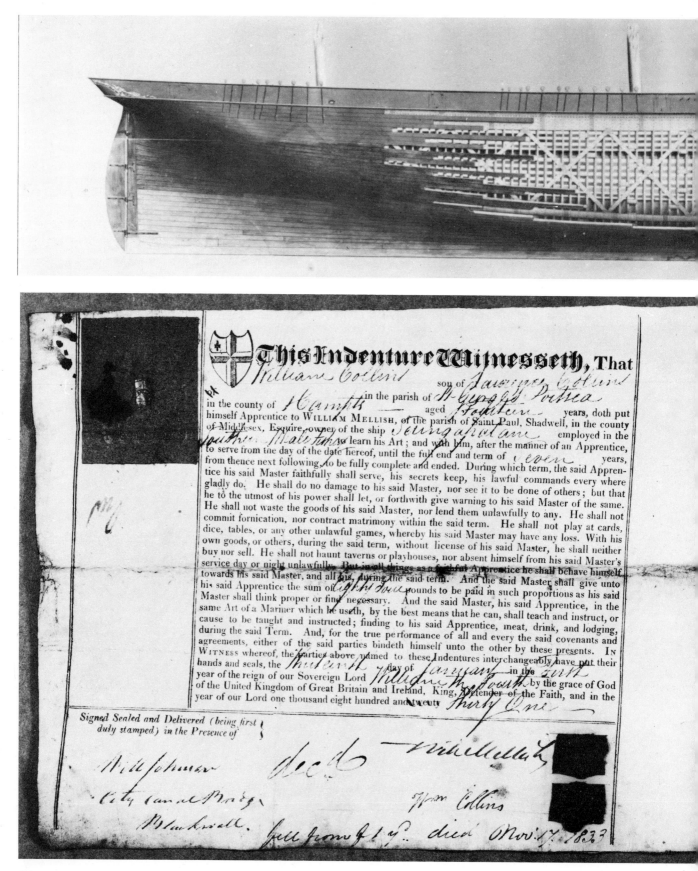

steerage were ironed and locked in the lazaret where they remained until handed over to the American authorities, charged with the crime of ravishing three young innocent girls, not one of them more than fifteen years of age.'

Even allowing for a certain amount of Irish blarney, it would still seem to have been a pretty hairy and unpleasant voyage. The handbill setting out the advantages of the *Marco Polo* for the Australia run sounded much more promising:

'Under engagement to sail from Liverpool, the splendid new frigate-built ship *Marco Polo*. A1 at Lloyd's of 1,622 tons burthen, copper-fastened throughout, now to make her first passenger voyage after sailing from New Brunswick, and her first to Australia. She is the largest, most commodious ship ever despatched from Liverpool on this service and is expected to sail as fast as any vessel afloat. She has ample accommodation for both passengers and freight, and will carry two experienced surgeons on board.'

The *Marco Polo* first sailed to Melbourne in 1850 carrying 930 passengers and thirty crew. She arrived in Port Philip Roads in sixty-eight days and made the passage back to Liverpool in seventy-six days, sailing up the Mersey flying under a banner which proclaimed her 'The Fastest Ship in the World'. On board she carried a 340-ounce gold nugget—a present to Queen Victoria from the Government of Victoria. She belonged to the famous Black Ball Line, which in its heyday employed 3,000 men and 300 officers in eighty-six ships.

American shipowners and American ships dominated the maritime scene for the first half of the nineteenth century—it was estimated that in 1860 American ships were carrying two-thirds of the world's trade. Then a year later the American Civil War broke out and during the next five years the cream of the cargo fleet was destroyed. The British

had not been idle since the repeal of the Navigation Acts, however, and Richard Green, a London ship-owner, made a fighting speech in London in 1850:

'We have heard recently a great deal about the dismal and doleful prospects of British shipbuilding and British shipping generally, we have heard, also, much about the British Lion and the American Eagle and the way in which they may find means of lying down together. I know little or nothing about this, but this much I do know—British shipowners are ready to take the Americans on at their own game, and I have an idea that we might one day beat them at it.'

He then promptly ordered the *Challenger*, of 1,000 tons, to be built for the tea trade. In 1852 she beat the American *Challenge* by two days on the run from Sunda Strait (between Java and Sumatra) to Deal, although the American made the faster passage from Canton to London by eight days. It is interesting to note that the British ship was almost exactly half the American's tonnage, and on the whole the British continued to build smaller ships than their competitors for the first few years of their 'freedom' from controls. It was not until the Aberdeen-built *Cairngorm* was launched in 1853 that they began to compare size for size.

There was another factor which, almost by accident, gave British shipbuilders the edge on the competition. Timber in America was cheap and plentiful, and this not only helped to expand the American marine but attracted foreign shipowners to build in America. But in Britain the demands of the Napoleonic wars had enormously depleted the available supplies of timber for shipbuilding so other means of construction were needed—and iron was plentiful. Iron ships were in fact built as far back as 1818, and the East India Company had an experimental brig and a barque built—the *Guide* and *John Laird*—in 1840. The *Lord of the Isles,* an early

The 1100-ton clipper ship *Sussex*, built in 1852, a lithograph by T. G. Dutton. The *Sussex* illustrates the practice of painting false gun-ports which lasted until late into the nineteenth century. National Maritime Museum, Greenwich.

British clipper, was an iron ship although iron was not favoured for the tea trade because it was thought to taint the cargo.

So the 'composite' ship, with iron frames and wooden planking, came into being. This had two advantages. The first was the obvious one of strength, giving greater rigidity and increased cargo space. The other was that it got round the problem that weed grows well on iron. Ships, particularly those for use in warmer weedier seas, had been sheathed in copper for many years to discourage the growth of weed, but you could not sheathe an iron ship, so to clothe an iron frame in wood and cover it in copper was a logical step. However, the paint manufacturers were not idle in the nineteenth century and reasonably effective anti-fouling compounds for treating the hulls of iron ships had been developed and were in use by the 1880s.

Big clipper ships were beautiful; they were also profitable. Sam Hall of Boston built the *Surprise* (1,361 tons) for Low. She sailed from New York for San Francisco under Captain Dumaresq with a crew of four mates, thirty able seamen, six ordinary seamen, two boatswains, four boys, two cooks, and a steward, a sailmaker and a carpenter. She also carried 18,000 tons of freight valued at a quarter of a million dollars. She had a pleasure cruise of a passage to San Francisco, reefing her topsails only twice on the voyage. After unloading she sailed, in ballast, to Canton where she loaded with tea at $25 the ton and had another uneventful passage back to New York. At the end of the round trip she had not only paid her cost and her keep but had made her owners a profit of $50,000–not a bad year's work. The *Staghound,* built by Donald McKay before the *Flying Cloud,* had a harder time on her first voyage and lost her main topmast and all three top-gallant masts six days out of New York; but she sailed on to California and then to Canton, via Manila, and had paid for herself and made her owners $8,000 on her return. The grain trade from the Pacific coast ports to Western Europe favoured the big square-riggers and it has been estimated that in the four years from 1881 to 1885 some three and three-quarter million pounds were

The 1625-ton clipper ship *Marco Polo* in the Mersey River, 1853, a lithograph by T. Dove. Outward bound to Melbourne—68 days; Melbourne to Liverpool—76 days: well-worthy of the title 'The Fastest Ship in the World'. National Maritime Museum, Greenwich.

earned by the fifteen hundred ships engaged in working that trade.

One cannot speak of clipper ships without some mention of the *Thermopylae* and the *Cutty Sark,* although every aspect of their history must have been written and re-written many times before. The *Thermopylae* was built first, in 1868, a composite ship of 991 tons registered, 210 feet long, 36 feet beam and 21 feet deep. Her value, apart from the sweetness of her lines, lay in the strength of her construction, which allowed her to be driven to the limit in the blustery Roaring Forties. Also, being small and light in comparison with the American two and a half thousand tonners, she could go well in light airs. It was this consistency of average speed that made her passages and those of her arch-rival, the *Cutty Sark,* so remarkable. On her maiden voyage the *Thermopylae* made a record passage of sixty-two days from the Lizard to Melbourne; she loaded with coal at Newcastle, New South Wales, and sailed for Shanghai on 10 February, arriving thirty-one days later. She then loaded with tea (her biggest tea cargo, on a later

voyage, was 1,429,000 pounds) and sailed from Foochow to the Lizard in eighty-nine days. Later, like the *Cutty Sark,* she was transferred to the wool run, which is where they both really made their names for remarkably short passages. The *Thermopylae* was sold to the Portuguese Government as a training ship in the 1890s and was finally towed to sea and sunk by torpedoes in 1907.

The *Cutty Sark* was built at Dumbarton for the specific purpose of beating the Aberdonian *Thermopylae.* She was almost identical in size, being 212 feet 5 inches long, 36 feet beam and 21 feet deep. On her maiden voyage in 1870, her mainmast measured 145 feet 9 inches from deck to truck. When on the tea run she never beat the *Thermopylae,* although she put up consistently fast passages of between 107 and 122 days. In 1872 she lost her rudder off the Cape coast while leading her rival; on that voyage she had done three consecutive days' sailing of 340, 327, and 320 miles. This gives an average speed, for those three days, of nearly fourteen knots. It has been calculated that the *Cutty Sark's* sail plan was

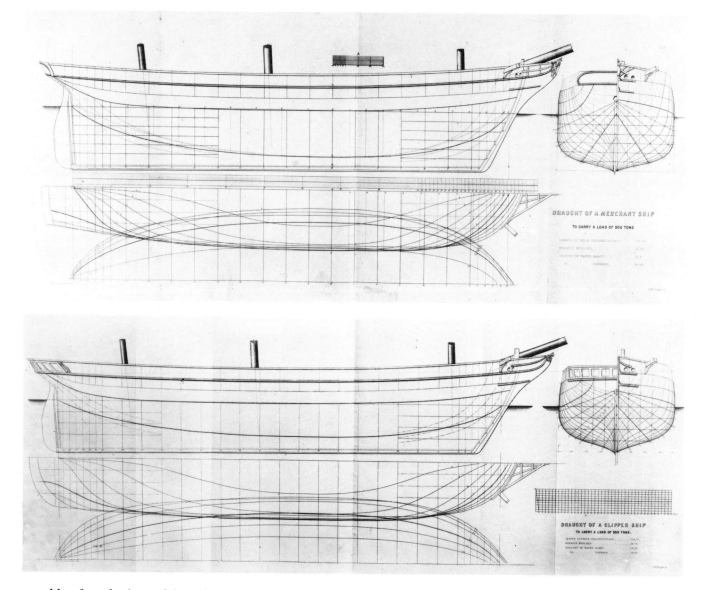

DRAUGHT OF A MERCHANT SHIP
TO CARRY A LOAD OF 500 TONS

DRAUGHT OF A CLIPPER SHIP
TO CARRY A LOAD OF 500 TONS.

capable of producing a drive of some three thousand horse power. As a comparison, a modern coastal merchantman of a similar size – 1,000 tons – would have maybe a one-thousand horse-power diesel engine and be capable of some twelve knots. From the point of view of speed the clippers put up remarkable figures, some of the big American clippers averaging over eighteen knots on a day's run. It is difficult to adjust one's thinking to the sizes of sailing vessels – Columbus discovered America in three ships not much longer than a rowing eight, and you could get five *Cutty Sarks* end-to-end on what would now be considered quite a moderate giant tanker.

The *Cutty Sark* was taken off the China run in 1878 and her sail plan cut down in 1880 while she plied for general cargoes round the world. In 1883 she joined the *Thermopylae* in the Australian wool trade where, for the next twelve years, she regularly

made incredibly fast passages – eighty-two days in 1884, eighty days in 1885 (when she beat the *Thermopylae* by a week), and in 1888 she took only sixty-nine days to the Lizard. As her skipper got to know her better he was able to cram more cargo aboard, too; and from 4,289 bales of wool in 1883 he increased her load to 5,304 bales in 1894. She was sold in 1895 and sailed under the Portuguese flag until 1922, working the well-worn Atlantic triangle Lisbon, Rio de Janeiro, New Orleans and back to Lisbon. She is now, thanks in great part to public interest and generosity, preserved in dry dock at Greenwich as a permanent museum and memorial to the last, most spectacular age of ocean-going sail.

Towards the end of the nineteenth century the hulls of all large ships were wholly of iron, or steel, construction and the use of steel went as far as masts, yards and rigging. These ships could no longer

Bottom: *Flying Cloud,* East Boston, Massachusetts, 1840. One of the famous early American clippers, she demonstrates the incredible spread of canvas carried. This was made even harder to handle because the topsails were not yet divided into two smaller sails. National Maritime Museum, Greenwich.

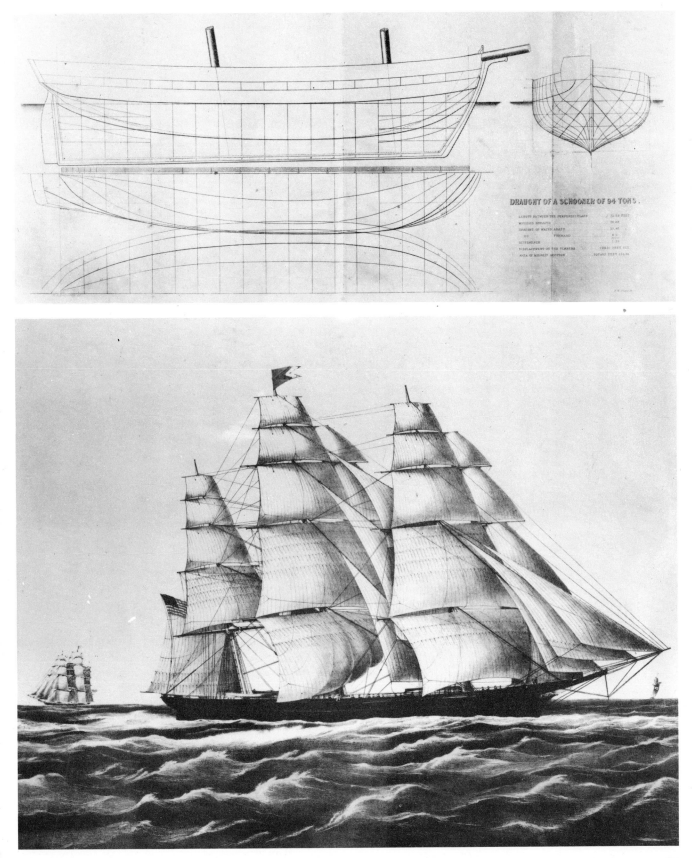

DRAUGHT OF A SCHOONER OF 94 TONS.

Four splendid figureheads from sailing
ships: (*top*) 'Old Turk' of the *Bosphorus*,
which was built as a brigantine and
lengthened into a three-master; (*bottom*)
Volunteer, which came from a coasting
vessel that carried coal to the Scilly Isles;

(*opposite top*) 'Spanish Lady', from an
unknown wreck on the Scillies; and
(*opposite bottom*) *Chieftain*, from a ship
wrecked on Hard Lewis in 1856. Lt.
Commander T. M. Dorrien Smith, Tresco
Abbey, Scilly Isles.

compete with steam for cargoes which demanded
rapid and predictable transport but they had a place
in the economic carriage of bulk cargo such as grain,
ore and nitrates. The great majority were now rigged
as barques–that is a vessel with at least three, and
often four, masts of which the aftermost–the mizzen–
is fore-and-aft rigged and the remainder are square
rigged. In 1902 the Germans launched the only five-
masted full-rigged ship ever built, a full-rigged ship
having square sails on all her masts. The *Preussen*
was 407 feet long and over 50 feet in beam. But, by and
large, the day of the square-rigger was over and what
sailing ships were built had to make the most
economical use of manpower. That meant a fore-and-
aft rig like the big American schooners–which were
trading up to 1939–or, more commonly in Europe,
barquentines which kept their square sails on only
the foremast, for running down the trades.

What has been left us from the age of the great
sailing traders is a mass of myth and legend shot
through with truth. There are stories of owners and
masters and mates, stories of mutinous crews, of
unbearable hardship and uneatable food, and stories
of ships with a will of their own and of winds, seas
and rocks to confound any geographer–and some of
them are true. Not all the stories are about men,
however, and not all the ladies in them are ships.

In March 1897, three months overdue, the *T. F.
Oakes* was towed into New York harbour by the
British tanker *Kasbek*. The *Oakes* was an iron-hulled
vessel registered as 1,997 tons and built for W. H.
Starbuck in Philadelphia in 1883. She was built for
capacity rather than speed as her maiden voyage from
New York to San Francisco showed; she took 195
days over the passage, nearly twice the average.

On her disastrous voyage home from Hong Kong
in 1896–7 she carried a crew of twenty-one seamen
commanded by Captain E. W. Reed and three mates;
the captain's wife, a strong, independent woman of
fifty who had sailed with her husband across the
world for many years, was also on board. They sailed
on the morning of 5 July in fine weather with lightish,
variable winds which enabled them to make slow
progress towards the Sunda Strait between Java and
Sumatra. However, 12 July dawned overcast and
sultry with the barometer steadily falling and all the
signs of a typhoon; and this was while the *Oakes* was
among the mass of tiny islands and dangerous reefs to
the east of Vietnam.

Captain Reed shortened sail to lower topsails and
hove-to to await the wind. It came. It came shrieking
out of a sultry calm and rapidly built up from nothing
to some eighty knots. The *T. F. Oakes* always hove-to
badly and all that day and night she lay uneasily with
the seas breaking the length of the deck; by morning
her fore and mizzen topmasts were sprung and half
her hatch covers had been torn away. Reed decided to
turn and run before the wind. For two days she ran

before the southwesterly in fine style – but the wrong direction; and she found herself off Formosa where she was caught by a second blow – this time from the north west. Running before this took her through the Balintang Channel and out into the Pacific.

Having been blown so far off course, in fact in completely the opposite direction, Reed decided to sail for New York round the Horn rather than the Cape of Good Hope. August, September and October all produced light, fickle winds in the Pacific that year and the *Oakes* was only off the Tuamotu archipelago, east of Tahiti, by the beginning of November. The crew by this time were getting pretty mutinous as water was short (and stagnant) and food was rank and nauseating in the continuous tropical heat. By the time that she rounded the Horn, 21 December 1896, two-thirds of the crew were laid up with scurvy, leaving only six hands on deck while Mrs Reed took a regular trick at the wheel.

By the beginning of February seven men had died, including the first mate, and the starved remains of the crew begged the captain to put in to Pernambuco, two days sail to the west. But Captain Reed stubbornly refused to change course to 'put himself in the hands of a lot of damned Dagoes ashore'. Two thousand miles further north, off Trinidad, they fell in with the *Governor Robie,* who was able to let them have some provision. Two days later, however, Captain Reed had a stroke and was confined, paralysed, to his cabin. This left the command of the ship to the inexperienced second mate and the captain's wife, who next met westerly gales off the Bahamas and were blown deep into the North Atlantic. They were just considering whether to abandon all hope of reaching New York and to bear away and run for Gibraltar when they fell in with the *Kasbek,* a British oil tanker, 600 miles east of New York. When the mate of the *Kasbek* boarded the *Oakes* in response to the distress flares they had been burning, he found that only the emaciated second mate and the redoubtable Mrs Reed were keeping the deck. These two were so exhausted that they were in no condition to haggle over the salvage charges involved in turning a loaded tanker around in mid-Atlantic to tow her to port – it was not yet possible to radio ashore for a tug. But their difficulties were not over: first they fouled the *Kasbek's* screw with the tow-line and then a gale blew up which prevented them making fast the tow again for three days. She was finally taken in tow on 18 March, 1897, and arrived in New York three days later after a voyage of 260 days. Lloyds presented Mrs Reed with their Silver Medal for Meritorious Service and Captain Reed was acquitted of charges of cruelty and incompetence. It is difficult to see, however, why he did not put into port at various stages of the voyage to obtain fresh food and medical supplies. One possibility put forward is that he was convinced that

Opposite top: The 1012-ton *Hurunui,* Lyttelton, New Zealand. This photograph of the New Zealand Shipping Company's full-rigged ship, the *Hurunui,* leaving the graving dock in January 1883 was presented to her 11,275-ton successor in April 1949.

Below left: The 1431-ton *Agamemnon,* the largest three-masted ship ever built at Blackwall, was launched in 1855. Comparison with the *Falmouth* (page 48) shows her to be less rounded and less decorated–built purely for profit with no display. National Maritime Museum, Greenwich.

Below right: The *Cutty Sark.* Taken by Captain Woodget in 1886 as the ship lay becalmed, this photograph shows the *Cutty Sark's* reduced rig. Her rig was cut down in 1880 when she came off the China run. She now lies preserved in a dry dock at Greenwich.

his crew would desert and could not face the thought of his owners having to send out a fresh crew; another is that, later, he was too sick to be able to make rational decisions. Whatever the cause, this disastrous voyage does show how difficulties at sea can accumulate–particularly when aided and abetted by a fairly inept master and crew.

Another sea-going lady, Elizabeth Wayth, has left her autobiography as the daughter, wife and mother of seamen. She went to sea as a baby and continued until she herself was carrying a child. Her description of life at sea is, naturally, filled with tales of storm, disaster and heroism. 'Naturally', because these make more interesting reading than the placid record of an uneventful voyage. Between voyages the wives and children went ship-visiting and Elizabeth remarks that, 'The most flimsy excuse was sufficient for a boat to be lowered and manned by apprentices, equally as eager for a visit to the half-deck of another ship.'

Amongst other types of craft, she describes the Deal 'hovellers', which piloted ships round the Goodwins and into the London river. They also increased their earnings by stripping any ship

unfortunate enough to run aground in the vicinity. Elizabeth Wayth's friend Frank Bullen, mate of the *Harbinger,* wrote, 'They are the finest boatmen in the world.' He tells a story of being bound up Channel and round the coast to Dundee when they were befogged off Beachy Head. 'A hoveller came alongside and made a bargain to take us to Dungeness for ten pounds. By the time he had scrambled on board our Captain began to wonder whether he might be available to pilot us right round to Dundee, not feeling very confident in his own knowledge of the East coast. So he put the question to our visitor, who replied that he himself was not qualified, and indeed would not be allowed to take us if he were. But he could arrange to have a North Sea pilot out in Deal Roads awaiting our arrival there. This was too much for our skipper's power of belief. That a cockle-shell of a lugger was able to outstrip his 1,400-ton ship with this breeze behind her, so much in forty miles? It couldn't be done!

' "Never mind, sir," said the hoveller, "You make my money up to thirteen pound for the whole job, and if you have to wait in the Downs for your pilot, you needn't pay me more than ten."

Below: The British Sail Training Association's *Sir Winston Churchill*, built in 1965. Every year hundreds of young men and women learn the skills involved in handling a three-masted schooner.

Opposite top: 'Ploddy' Erikson's ill-fated *Pamir* off Falmouth in the autumn of 1949. This fully-rigged barque was lost with only six survivors in 1957.

Opposite bottom: The United States of America's sail training ship *Eagle*. This three-masted bark is well-known in Europe as she regularly takes part in the famous 'Tall Ships Race' against her fellows from Europe and South America.

Loading a ship with squared timber through a bow port, Quebec, 1872. The timber, squared at the logging camps hundreds of miles inland, was too cumbersome to load through hatches. Notman Photographic Archives, McCord Museum of McGill University, Montreal.

The *Lucile,* Union Street wharf, San Francisco, 1901. This 1402-ton vessel was the last ship in San Francisco to be hove down—to clean and repair her underwater body. She was lost, together with $186,000-worth of canned and pickled salmon, in 1908. San Francisco Maritime Museum, California.

' "It's a go," answered the Captain, fully satisfied.

'Hailing his boat, the Dealman gave his instruction. Crowding on all sail, away she went, sheering in for the shore, and soon was lost to sight in the mist. Meanwhile we made all the sail she would carry, and made a fairly rapid run to the Downs. Sure enough there was a galley punt awaiting us, the men lying on their oars, and the pilot with his bag lounging in the stern.'

These hovellers would meet a ship to get a pilot on board under any conditions, and they would go after salvage when even the lifeboats would turn back, as Miss Wayth says, 'Not under any pretence of philanthropy, but in the hope of earning something', but she continues that, 'It may be gratefully recorded that they never shirk the most dreadful risks when there is a hope of saving life.'

The last great sailing shipowner was Gustav Erikson—known, more or less affectionately, as 'Ploddy Erikson' to his seamen. He went to sea in North Sea coasters at the age of nine and commanded one by the time he was twenty. He then spent six years as mate in deep-water ships and from 1902 to 1913 he was the master of a square-rigger. After the war he became a shipowner, sending a fleet of sailing ships out of Mariehamn at the mouth of the Gulf of Bothnia in the Baltic to the Great Australian Bight for grain. This trade was the last stronghold of sail before the 1939–45 war, it not being considered profitable to send a steamship up the 180-mile long

inlet of the Spencer Gulf to the heart of the Australian wheat belt. There was no import trade and the ships had therefore to sail out in ballast and then wait, sometimes for two months, for a cargo.

The Spencer Gulf lies only 5° north of the Roaring Forties and almost exactly midway round the world from Europe. The grain ships set out at the end of September in ballast to pick up the north and south-east trades until they were south of Tristan da Cunha. Then they ran down the westerlies in the latitude 40° south, sailing out of the South Atlantic, below the Cape of Good Hope and on across the southern Indian Ocean until they picked up the South Neptune Islands off the mouth of the Spencer Gulf. This was often the first landfall they made during the entire three-month voyage.

Having arrived off the Gulf they had then to wait until a cargo was arranged, and this could take weeks. When one was finally laid on, the next job was to unload the sand ballast onto the ballast grounds. This was done by hand, shovelling the sand into buckets and slinging it overside through special ports cut low in the side. The ship was then worked

up the shallow gulf to the station from which it was to receive the cargo. At Port Germein there was a jetty over a mile long; at most other places the grain had to be loaded from lighters. Sixty-thousand-odd sacks of grain hauled up, swung in, lowered and then stowed, made warm work for the crews who consisted, between the wars, mostly of young candidates for second mates' tickets doing their statutory three years in sail. The grain ships left, normally, around the beginning of March and arrived in Falmouth towards the end of June. They then went into dry dock either at the port of discharge or back in the Baltic at Mariehamn to prepare for the next trip six months later.

The crews, who as I said were mostly embryo second mates with a stiffening of old seamen, were paid the princely sum of 600 Finnmarks a month. That was then worth about three pounds. The captain, 'master under God' of the ship, crew and cargo, was paid £20 a month – but Erikson had no great difficulty in finding candidates. In spite of these obvious economies, the grain fleet which numbered sixty ships in 1921 had shrunk to fourteen in 1929.

Opposite: The *Vencateswaraloo*, a trading ship from the Indian Ocean. These under-canvassed but easily-handled sailing ships are still scraping a living trading between the remote islands of the Indian Ocean.

Below: The Baltic ketch *Seute Deern*. Chartered from the famous shipping line Norddeutschen Lloyd, she is the training ship of the Deutschen Reederverbander.

Below: On board the *Pamir* in 1939. This photograph underlines the fact that without steam sail-driven ships were powered by muscle in the final analysis.

Opposite top: A Pacific coast barkentine, *circa* 1912. The 1040-ton *Thomas P. Emigh,* built in 1901, still holds the record for the fastest passage between Honolulu and the Coast (7 days 22 hours). She foundered off the California coast in 1932. San Francisco Maritime Museum, California.

Opposite bottom: A three-masted bark, the *Star of Finland*. Barks had fore-and-aft rigging on only the mizzen, and this is the largest example ever built in the United States. She was steel-built in Maine in 1899 for the Pacific trade. San Francisco Maritime Museum, California.

Chapter seven

Coastal traffic

The last stronghold

The age of the large merchant sailing ship is now over, even the most sentimental owner cannot afford to preserve an unprofitable memory–and shipowners are not known for their soft-heartedness in commerce. In Europe, coastal craft, too, are a vanishing sight but sail is still holding its own, just, in the West Indian and Pacific trading schooners and Chinese coasting junks. There is still a great quantity of sailing river craft east of Suez with names like badan, patile, twaqo, prahu and caracor. The names of the old European coastal and fishing vessels are, in many ways, as curious-sounding to the landsman's ear: smack, bawley, hoy, aak, hekjalk, fifey, and quay punt.

Properly to discuss or describe even a moderate fraction of the coastal sailing craft of Europe–or of Britain alone–would take more than one entire book. No more can be done here than briefly to touch upon the types of boat generally found in European coastal waters and to describe one or two in more detail.

The major difference between coastal and deep-sea sailing is that when sailing the oceans one is normally sailing down-wind, whereas in coastal waters this 'downhill' sailing is a bonus, not the rule. The climate of the world is such that there is a belt of predominantly westerly winds below each pole with the north-east trades above the equator and the south-east trades below. This pattern means, in broad terms, that it is possible to travel the world with the wind on your beam or behind you. This is why Chay Blyth's historic voyage in *British Steel* was described as 'going round the wrong way'. Such a voyage would have been nearly impossible in a square-rigged ship. It often happened, in fact, that Australian square-rigged coasters wishing to sail from, say, Sydney to Perth would find it quicker to sail eastwards round the Horn and on round the world rather than the two thousand-odd miles round the coast.

But, of course, this principle does not operate in coastal waters and therefore coastal shipping has to be able to make to windward efficiently and has also to be very manoeuvrable to navigate in confined spaces. This means a fore-and-aft rig. We have seen that the Portuguese caravels, which were developed from fishing boats, were rigged with a 'lateen' sail–a triangular sail with a long yard along the top. This was the earliest form of fore-and-aft rig and, as its name suggests (it is a corruption of 'Latin'), it was

found in the Mediterranean. It completely superseded the square sail in those waters from about the fourth to the fourteenth century. This rig was associated with all the countries under the influence of the Islamic Empire but its origin is still unknown. It is a most attractive and quite efficient rig but does suffer the disadvantage that the very long yard has to be handed round the mast to the new leeward side at every tack. (Tacking is the zig-zag fashion in which a sailing boat makes to windward.) By shortening the yard and making the sail a trapezium rather than a triangle, this operation is simplified and the sail becomes a 'dipping lug'. 'Dipping', because the sail has to be dipped round the mast at each tack. Greatly shortening the yard so that only a fraction of the sail projected in front of the mast produced a 'standing lug', and the sail could be left alone when tacking. This rig, however, always sailed better on one tack than the other.

The dipping lug was the most common form of sail in Britain for all small fishing vessels from the Kentish to the Scottish coasts. It was the rig used in those small, handy vessels which took pilots and some passengers on or off ships arriving at, or leaving, our coasts, and it was a favoured rig for the bands of English and French smugglers who did not see why minor disturbances like wars should affect honest trade.

The Dutch developed a different form of fore-and-aft sail, the 'spritsail'. This was a rectangular sail with a long edge attached up and down the mast and the sail supported by a spar (or sprit) running diagonally from the foot of the mast to the outer top corner of the sail. It was the form of sail found on Thames barges, the last of which has only recently stopped working for her living, and was an easy sail to handle because it did not have to be lowered to furl it nor did hands have to go aloft to gather it. All that needed to be done was to lower the head of the sail down the mast–which coped with the sail above the sprit–and then draw the portion below the sprit up by brails. The spritsail did not project in front of the mast. This meant that it was possible to rig a supporting stay–the forestay–from the top of the mast to the bow of the boat. On this stay it was possible to set a new sail, the forestaysail, the triangular sail seen on all modern yachts and familiar as the foresail, or (wrongly in fact) the jib. Although

Lateen Rig
This rig originated in the
Mediterranean early in the
Christian era and still
maintains its usefulness –
particularly on the Tagus and
in the Persian Gulf.

Dipping Lug
The basic rig of both French and British
small coastal shipping for hundreds of
years.

Spritsail Barge
Thames barges were the last bastion of coastal
sail in Europe. The rig is efficient and
economical – an eighty-foot barge could be
handled by two men.

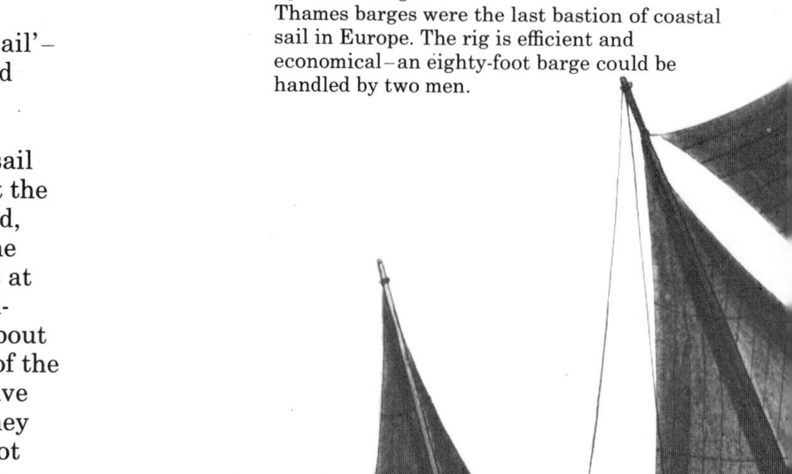

it was certainly not recognised at the time, this was
an enormous step forward: the efficiency of a fore-
and-aft rig is in great part due to the 'slot' effect of
the wind passing between the two sails, giving
increased lift.

The third form of fore-and-aft sail – the 'gaff sail' –
developed from the lateen mizzen of three-masted
ships. Somewhere about the beginning of the
eighteenth century the part of the lateen sail in
front of the mast was done away with, giving a sail
longer in the leech than in the luff (i.e. longer at the
back than in the front) with a yard at the top and,
later, a boom along the bottom. In small ships the
yard soon became a genuine gaff, ending in jaws at
the mast, but the larger naval ships kept the full-
length lateen yard as a useful spare spar until about
1800. *Vanguard*, Nelson's flagship at the battle of the
Nile, was rigged this way. The Dutch seem to have
achieved the gaff rig via two separate routes. They
went from a spritsail to a half sprit which was not
lowered and had the sail brailed up to it, or they
appear to have derived it from the lateen sail by
up-ending it so that the yard became the mast and
adding a short, curved spar at the top to help it stand.
The net result in each case is a recognizable gaff
mainsail. This gaff rig became the most popular rig
for all coasting vessels over a certain size, excluding
the Thames barges, Norfolk wherries and their like.

Standing Lug
A modification on the dipping lug,
it is not so efficient but it is easier
to handle as the yard does not have
to be handed round the mast at
each tack.

Gaff Yawl
The traditional rig of coastal
smacks and trawlers.

Below: The Blackwater Barge Match, Essex, July 1966. Although no working barges survive, many are still kept up by individuals and clubs. Nearly all turn out for the various barge races which are the highlight of their season.

Opposite top: A Leith smack running 'swin' with all sail set, 19 October, 1838, by J. Schetky. This smack, carrying passengers and cargo south from Scotland, has set everything but the skipper's shirt to try to catch the tide up the Thames. National Maritime Museum, Greenwich.

Opposite bottom: A Bristol Channel pilot cutter. The strength and sea-keeping quality of this tough old lady (now re-rigged as a ketch) is still evident in spite of her age.

A mortgage agreement for the versatile *Harmony*, employed in fishing, carrying passengers, dredging and attending shipping between Harwich and Portsmouth, dated September 1829. Greater London Record Office, on loan from Messrs Farrer and Company, London.

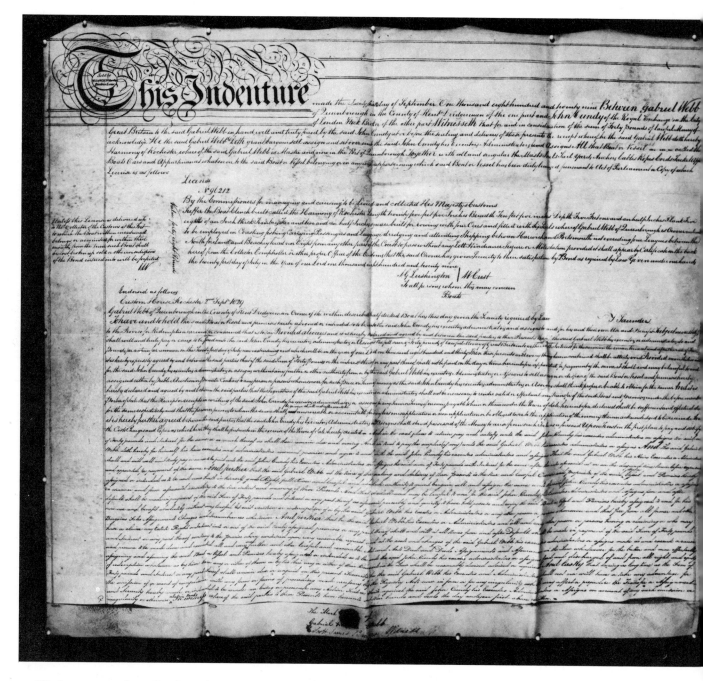

We have seen that the Americans used this rig extensively in their schooners—which ran up to the *Thomas W. Lawson*'s 5,000 tons. In Europe schooners were also very popular for the coastal trade, but they were of much more modest proportions, a hundred odd tons was the rule rather than the exception. These schooners were found all round the coasts of Europe, most particularly, perhaps, in the Baltic. What is more there are still some working schooners in the Baltic, and the little schooners that brought china clay round from the Cornish ports to the London river finally vanished in the Second World

War. These schooners, gaff-rigged on both masts with a square topsail on the foremast, could be handled by the traditional 'two men and a boy'—although I discovered to my disappointment too many years ago that the 'boy' was a strapping youth of eighteen not a schoolboy of eight.

At that time, in the middle 'thirties, inshore fishing boats were still driven by sail and there was a fleet of some twenty oyster smacks at Whitstable alone. These smacks were cutter rigged, that is they had an enormous gaff mainsail with the boom stretching well out over the counter with a fore-and-aft topsail above.

In front of the mast they carried a forestaysail and, set on a moveable bowsprit, a jib and, on occasion, a jib-topsail. They had a vertical stem and a long straight keel which helped them to windward and made them very steady in a sea. They had a very bold sheer and a long, low counter to facilitate the handling of their trawling gear. Ramsgate smacks, just round the corner of Kent, were larger vessels which fished the North Sea and had cut up their sail plan into more manageable pieces by reducing the mainsail and giving themselves a mizzen. Smacks were also used for the coastal carriage of passengers and cargo, and the Leith smack offered a faster and, given fair weather, more pleasant alternative to the stage coach for the four hundred mile journey from Edinburgh to London. This service was finally killed in about 1840 by the coming of the steam railway.

The Thames barges, however, soldiered on until Bob Roberts, ex-policeman, journalist and the last barge-master, finally hung up his hat in the late 1960s. They had been dwindling fast before that, 'though, and like so many things really went out with the

1939–45 war. In her final form the Thames barge has had some two hundred years of life – that is as a sprit-sailed, flat-bottomed, bluff-bowed boat with leeboards. These last, always associated with barges and Dutch 'boiers' and 'botters', are large hinged 'flaps' which can be lowered down the side of the hull to prevent it sliding sideways to leeward. The lines of an English chalk barge are illustrated in Chapman's *Architectura Navalis Mercatoria*, published in 1768, and show a swim-bowed, flat-bottomed hull some 56 feet overall, 15 feet wide and 5 feet deep, with a single mast and leeboards. Steel's *Rigging and Seamanship* of 1794 describes the sails and rigging of sailing barges and lighters, and these remained practically unchanged until the present day. As barges became longer a mizzenmast was added – sometime in the 1820s – which made for ease of handling in the narrow limits of the London river. A little later topsails were added to some of the larger craft and two distinct sorts of barge emerged: the 'stumpy' barges without topsails which plied the Thames, and the 'topsail' barges which worked the coastal trade.

The shipwreck by Joseph Mallord
William Turner (1775–1851). A dramatic
picture of disaster at sea painted with
enormous gusto and relish. The Tate
Gallery, London.

Below: A model of the smack *Comet*, 1809. Smacks carried goods and passengers down the East Coast in the nineteenth century and were still fishing regularly up to 1939. Science Museum, London.

Opposite: An old East Indiaman on Northfleet Hope, 1787. One of Roy George's smacks from Gravesend lies-to with her mainsail 'scandalized' aft. National Maritime Museum, London.

The latter were not river craft but well-found sea-going vessels, sailing to Falmouth, Brest, up the Humber, across to Holland and round Land's End to Ireland. In the 1890s the *Davenport* sailed to the Shetlands, and Captain Garnham sailed the *Eastern Belle* out of Pin Mill to Lisbon and back.

Barges succeeded in resisting the threat of steam and motor ships because they were perfectly designed for the job they had to do. They were economical in manpower, ran on 'free' air, and were of such shallow draught that they could visit coastal harbours that were closed to all other load-carrying traffic. Hay barges even sailed up the narrow creeks of coastal and estuary farms and then sailed down again like floating haystacks, a man perched on top to act as the steerman's eyes, with feed for the carriage and dray horses of London. Another class of barge common in the middle of the nineteenth century was the 'sandy'. This was a small barge used for dredging scouring sand for scrubbing floors and tables. The sandies were traditionally supposed to supplement their income by sheep stealing from the saltings lining the Thames and it was *de rigeur* when sailing past one to bleat and 'baa' at the crew – and then duck! The last known sandies had the temperate names of *Band of Hope* and *Blue Ribbon*.

In the middle 1920s Everard & Sons built four great steel barges at Yarmouth – the *Ethel, Fred, Alf* and *Will Everard*. They were 97 feet long, 23 feet beam and 9½ feet deep. They could carry 300 tons of cargo and were driven by over five and a half thousand square feet of canvas. In 1929 Captain E. Mole left Weymouth one Thursday at noon in the *Alf Everard*. He brought up in Hull by ten o'clock on the Saturday morning. Something over four hundred miles in forty-six hours would not be sneered at even

Opposite: Hay barges in an estuary, by
Richard Henry Nibbs (*circa* 1816–1893).
These barges, aground and waiting for the
tide, show the incredible bulk of deck
cargo that could be carried. Lowndes
Lodge Gallery, London, S.W.1.

Below: The sailing wherry *Albion* on the
River Yare in Norfolk. The *Albion* carried
a loose-footed gaff mainsail, whereas most
wherries favoured the spritsail rig of the
Thames barge.

if it were achieved under power, in a motor coaster.

Thames barges are, probably, nowadays chiefly
known for the annual Barge Race which was first
sailed officially in 1863 under the enthusiastic guidance
of Mr Henry Dodd. Mr Dodd, a well-known building
contractor, hoped that the races would not only
provide sport but would encourage owners and
builders to produce faster, handier craft. In 1865 a
second race was added to the programme, for the
'Championship of the Thames', also at the instance of
Henry Dodd. The first race produced the following
results: topsail barges–1st *Agnes,* 2nd *Surprise,*
3rd *Matilda and Amy;* stumpies–1st *Maria,* 2nd
Charles, 3rd *Elizabeth.* In the 'Championship' race a
fortnight later *Matilda and Amy* and *Maria* won their

classes. After the race the bargemen presented Dodd
with a handsome silver snuff-box inscribed:
'Presented to H. Dodd, Esqre., by bargemen, as a
token of respect and esteem, and in acknowledgement
of the interest he has taken in their welfare, Aug. 29,
1865.'

The most famous barge ever built was probably
Giralda, which was launched in 1897 and promptly
won the Jubilee Championship. She continued
winning races throughout her career, although she
was protested against on her first appearance as
being built for racing and not as a working ship. She
was, in fact, sent back to her builders and
strengthened after her first season–but this did not
upset her winning ways.

115

Chapter eight
Hazards at sea

If one goes to, say, the National Maritime Museum in London to study prints of merchant ships, they seem to fall into three categories of subject. The smallest section consists of landscapes of an estuary or port with titles like: 'A prospect of Barking Reach from Tripcock Point looking towards the Magazine'. There will be half a dozen barques and three barges sailing about and, in the foreground, a gentleman in an unlikely hat arguing with a boatman. The second section consists of rather stilted ship 'portraits', for example 'The Packet *Kate Simmons,* 1026 tons, on her Maiden Voyage to New York. Presented to Her Owners and Officers'. The third, and by far the largest, displays all sorts of maritime disasters with enormous relish and much romantic splendour of engulfing wave and towering thunderheads; these have titles explaining everything most exactly, such as: 'The Indiaman *Mark and Michael* wrecked off the Scillies, June 10th 1769, with 746 Men and Women on Board. The Sloop *Starfish* endeavour'd to give assistance but was dasht to Pieces in the Attempt. Not a Soul was Saved.' It speaks volumes for the courage of the public, for whose consumption these dramas were displayed, that people continued to travel by sea.

Life at sea is, of course, potentially hazardous and often frightening – as any challenge thrown down to such enormously powerful forces as wind and water must be. Ships are lost and so are lives, but very few in relation to the numbers who have ventured successfully. Pompey the Great, when warned of the dangers of putting to sea in the Mediterranean winter, brushed the sailor's words aside with: 'I must sail; I do not have to survive.' (*Navigare necesse est; vivere non est necesse.*)

The most widely publicized shipwreck is, I suppose, that of Saint Paul on the coast of Malta, reported in Chapter 27 of the Acts of the Apostles. This wreck provides an absolutely classic warning against navigating a square-rigged ship in confined waters at the wrong time of year – which was just what Saint Paul was complaining about when they set out from 'the fair havens; nigh whereunto was the the city of Lasea'. He must have been infuriating to carry because he was not even a passenger but a prisoner and he had a maddening habit of being right. Sure enough, as he had warned them, the southerly wind that they had hoped would take them to the

'more commodious' harbour of Phenice swung round to the east and blew up into a gale. Blown towards the west with no sight of the sun or stars to give them any idea of their position, it is not surprising that they ended in disaster. The sailors in the New Testament account do not show up at all well, either running up and down in panic wringing their hands or deciding to do quite the wrong thing. They did, however, actually save the ship. Verse 27 says, 'But when the fourteenth night was come . . . about midnight the shipmen deemed that they drew nigh to some country: and sounded and found it twenty fathoms: and when they had gone a little further they sounded again and found it fifteen fathoms. Then fearing lest we should have fallen upon rocks, they cast four anchors out of the stern, and wished for day.' They then reverted to form and tried to abandon both the ship and their passengers. I cannot believe that this was the normal standard of Mediterranean seamanship of the period.

What is certainly true is that a ship, provided that she is seaworthy to start with, can last a lot longer than her crew and it is man's mistakes – caused by fatigue, fear, ignorance or, as the owner of the *Edward Cotton* has it, 'through meere dissolute negligence' – that are responsible for the majority of maritime disasters.

Life at sea, even as late as the seventeenth century, was thought to be much more exciting than it is today because, apart from the normal hazards of winds, sea and rocks, the navigator had to contend with monsters capable of crushing the ship with one blow, the mountains of magnetic ore which could draw out all the fastenings of his ship, and whirlpools that could drag him down to the centre of the earth. His crew, too, were not entirely convinced that if you sailed too far in any direction you would not fall over the edge and into oblivion. But still, as with Saint Paul's adventure, the basic cause of most shipwrecks was faulty navigation. This is well exemplified by the report of the ten survivors of the *Tobie* – wrecked off the Barbary coast in 1593.

'The *Tobie* of London a ship of 250 tunnes manned with fiftie men, the owner whereof was the worshipfull M. Richard Staper, being bound for Livorno, Zante and Patras in Morea, being laden with merchandize to the value of 11 or 12 thousand pounds sterling, set sayle from Black-wall the 16 day of

116

cūmuſ ſe inpfundum ingant: tamen in natando repunt. un
ydaud air. hoc mare magnū & ſpaciofū manib; illic repti
lia q̄rū non eſt numer. Anphitria ſunt q̄dā genꝺa piſciū dc̄ta
q̄ꝺ ambulandi in cerriſ uſum ⁊ natandi in aquiſ officium
habeant. Anphi enī g̃ce. utrumq; dr̄.i. q̄a in aq̄ꝓ ⁊ⁱⁿ teⁿⁱs uiuunt.
ut phoce. cocodrilli. ⁊ypotami. hoc eſt equi fluctualeſ.

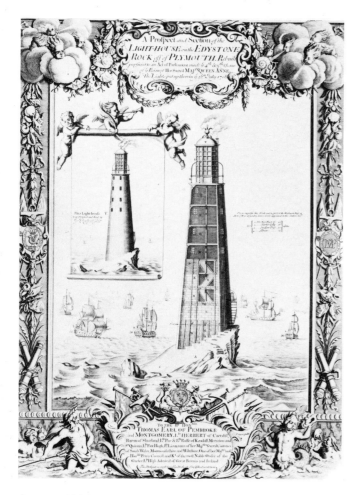

seamen Humphrey Gilbert and Walter Raleigh lost their flagship on 29 August, 1583, off Newfoundland. (In the following extract it must be borne in mind that the fleet was commanded by the General and that 'Admiral' means the flagship, not the man.)

'Upon Tewsday the 27 of August, toward the evening, our Generall caused them in his frigat to sound, who found white sand at 35 fadome, being then in latitude about 44 degrees.

'Wednesday toward night the wind came South, and wee bare with the land all the night, Westnorthwest, contrary to the mind of Master Cox (Master of the Golden Hind of 40 tons burthen): nevertheless wee followed the Admirall, deprived of power to prevent a mischiefe, which by no contradiction could be brought to hold other course, alleaging they could not make the ship to work better, nor to lie otherwaies.

'The evening was faire and pleasant, yet not without token of storme to ensue, and most part of this Wednesday night, like the Swanne that singeth before her death, they in the Admiral, or *Delight* [the name of the flagship], continued in sounding of Trumpets, with Drummes, and Fifes: also winding the Cornets, Haughtboyes: and in the end of their jolitie, left with the battell and ringing of doleful knells.

'Towards the evening also we caught in the Golden Hinde a very mighty Porpose, with a harpyng iron, having first stricken divers of them, and brought away part of their flesh, sticking upon the yron, but could not recover onely that one. These also passing through the Ocean, in herdes, did portend storme. I omit to recite frivolous reportes by them in the Frigat, of strange voyces, the same night, which scarred some from the helme.'

Shortly Master Cox saw breaking surf and, on sounding, they found that they were in among a mass of shoals, 'Amongst which we found shoale and deepe in every three or foure shippes length, after wee began to sound.'

'Immediately tokens were given to the *Delight,* to cast about to seaward, which, being the greater ship, and of burden 120 tunnes, was yet foremost in the breach, keeping so ill a watch, that they knew not the danger, before they felt the same, too late to recover it: for presently the Admirall strooke a ground, and soone after her stern and hinder partes beaten in pieces: whereupon the rest (that is to say, the Frigat in which was the Generall and the Golden Hinde) cast about Eastsoutheast, bearing to the South, even for our lives into the wind's eye, because that way carried us to the seaward.'

Nearly all the ship's company were lost, among them a learned Hungarian who was a notable poet and orator; they also lost 'Our Saxon Refiner and Discoverer of inestimable riches, as it was left amongst some of us in undouted hope' [whatever that might mean. P.J.B.].

August 1593 . . . we had sight of Mount Chiego, which is the first high-land which we descrie on the Spanish coast at the entrance of the Straight of Gibraltar, where we had very foule weather and the wind scant two days together. Here we lay off to sea. The Master, whose name was George Goodlay, being a young man, and one which never tooke charge before for those parts, was very proud of the charge which he was litle able to discharge, neither would take counsel of any of his company, but did as he thought best himselfe, & in the end of the two dayes of foule weather cast about, and the wind being faire, bare in with the straights mouth. The 19 day at night he thinking that he was farther off the land than he was, bare sayle all that night, & an houre and an halfe before day had ranne our shippe upon the ground on the coast of Barbarie . . . Whereupon being all not a little astonied, the Master said unto us, I pray you forgive me; for this is my fault and no man's else.' Of the fifty who sailed from Blackwall, only ten returned after being captured by the Moors and ransomed for £70 by the local English merchants.

It was not only the young and unknown mariners who found themselves in difficulty in that age of navigation by supposition. Those well-known Devon

The present State of the ABERGAVENNY in 10 Fathoms of Water & sunk 5 - 6 in Sand & Means using in recovering the Property on board.

Sept.r 29.th 1805.

1. Men on board the Boyne Sloop raising a Box of Copper.
2. D.o raising a Cable.
3. Men on a Scaffold sawing the Gun Deck.
4. The Diver directing & hoisting up Passenger's Chest out of Gun room.
5. Men on a Scaffold holding the Fan.
6. a Man on board the Ketch attending to the Directions of the Diver which are conveyed to him through an Air Tube.

7. Men holding the Rope by which the Diver is suspended.
8. Part of the upper Deck & Ends of the Beams where sawn off.
9. Remaining Part of the Gun Deck.
10. Opening to the after Hold.
11. an Opening cut thro' the Poop Deck Quarter Deck & Gun Deck.
12. Feet by it having taken the goods out of Gun room & now about making Way thro' Orlope Deck to the Money.

Dedicated by Permission to their Royal Highnesses the

The *Bay of Panama,* shipwrecked in March
1891 in a blizzard off Penare Point, Lizard,
in Cornwall with a loss of twenty lives,
including the skipper and his wife.
Seventeen men were saved by rocket and
'breeches buoy'.

Ships have been wrecked as long as there have
been ships to sail and land to wreck them on, and men
have been lost from them since before Jonah. One
man who was just as lucky as Jonah was an
anonymous sailor on board the famous American
clipper *Flying Cloud.* In 1855, while the ship was
doing 12 knots off the coast of Madagascar, the man
slipped and fell overboard. The only witness was
Mrs Cressey, the captain's wife, who was on deck at
the time. She raised the alarm and the *Flying Cloud*
put about and, under reduced canvas, searched the
sea back along her route. It was not until four hours
later that he was sighted, a boat lowered and a very
thankful seaman hauled aboard. It was in the same
part of the ocean, it will be remembered, that a
British East Indiaman picked up a Malay who had
been lost overboard from a Dutchman in March 1748
(see chapter four).

The toll of shipwrecks did not end with the
nineteenth century. The Scandinavian shipowner
Gustav Erikson had square-rigged sailing ships
trading at a profit right up to 1939, and as they
became old and tired several were lost. The *Herzogin
Cecilie* was one such example. An all-steel, 3,000-ton,
German-built four-masted barque, she was launched
in 1902, when she promptly made the passage from the
Lizard to Montevideo in only fifty-three days. During
the First World War she was interned at Coquimbo,

two hundred miles north of Valparaiso on the coast of
Chile. She was bought by Erikson for £4,000 and set
to work earning her living on the grain run–in 1927
she beat all her competitors by a full thirty days. Ten
years later she went aground off Soar Mile Cove,
west of Bolt Head in Devon, and was lost.

More recently still, the 2,799-ton *Pamir* was lost.
Another German-built ship bought by Erikson, she
was later sold back to her country of origin as a cadet
ship. In September 1957, with a cargo of grain and a
crew of thirty-five sailors and fifty-one cadets, she was
one thousand miles out of Buenos Aires when
she was caught by the tail of Hurricane Carrie. By
21 September she had developed a forty-degree list
and was still some six hundred miles south west of the
Azores. Two of the three inflatable lifeboats were put
out of action and twenty men scrambled into the
remaining one; twenty-three men managed to man
one standard lifeboat and ten the other. There were
six survivors from the crew of eighty-six–but as soon
as they had recovered their strength they all
volunteered to sail in the *Pamir*'s sister ship, the
Passat.

The sea is a hard mistress but she casts a spell
over men that they find hard to break–the more
particularly when they woo her with a sail-driven
ship rather than try to assert their will with the help
of engine-driven propellers.

Below: The *Jeune Hortense,* a brigantine wrecked off Eastern Green, Penzance, in 1888. The crew of three men and a boy were saved by the Penzance lifeboat *Dora* – seen rowing ashore.

Next page: The ship *Cromdale,* wrecked off the Lizard, 1913. When she struck, the crew took to the boats, later returning to collect their dunnage. She settled beneath them and they were rescued from the rigging by local lifeboats.

Glossary

Artemon A small, square sail set under the bowsprit to aid steering, developed by the Romans. Used until the eighteenth century and known as the 'spritsail', it is not to be confused with a barge's spritsail (q.v.).

Backstay plate The iron strap to which the backstay was fastened. The backstays led aft and counteracted the pull of the sails when the ship was running before the wind.

Ballast Heavy material placed low down in the ship to lower the centre of gravity and to keep the ship stable. A ship was 'in ballast' when it was without cargo and carried only gravel (still known as ballast) to keep her seaworthy.

Beak-head The planking of the ship run forward to support the bowsprit. It was often intricately decorated.

Beam The width of a ship. If used undefined it means the greatest width.

Bilges That part of the hull, or underwater body, of a ship upon which she would rest if aground.

Bolt ropes The edges of a sail are strengthened by sewing a rope into them.

Bonnet An extra piece of material laced to the foot of a square sail to increase its area in light winds.

Boom The spar running along the foot (bottom edge) of a sail to give firmer control of its shape.

Bowsprit The pole which ran more or less horizontally from the ship's bow and carried first the artemon, then the spritsails, and finally the jibs.

Brails Ropes running vertically from the foot of a sail which gather the sail up like a theatre curtain.

Bulwarks The 'walls' formed by the sides of the ship rising above the deck.

Carvel The method of construction in which the ship's planking is laid edge to edge giving a smooth surface.

Cat-head A beam projecting from the bows of a ship to form a simple crane for hauling up and stowing the anchor (from the Latin *catina*).

Clinker The method of construction in which a ship's planking is laid so that each plank overlaps the one below.

Compass rose *See* Rose

Counter That part of the stern of a ship which extends from the waterline to the full outward swell.

Courses The lowest, and largest, of the square sails set on any mast. Main course is equivalent to mainsail, etc.

Cutwater An extra piece of timber added to the front of the stem of a ship. Its function was partly protective and partly to increase the effective length of the keel.

Davit The miniature 'cranes' for lowering or hoisting boats into the water from a ship.

Deadeye A round laterally flattened block of wood, pierced with holes through which a lanyard is reeved, used to extend shrouds (q.v.).

Draught The depth between the waterline and the bottom of the keel. *cf.* Draw

Draw A ship that draws ten feet of water needs a depth of water of ten feet to float. *cf.* Draught

Foresail In a ship with more than one mast the lowest sail set on the forward mast. The triangular sail set on the forestay of a ship, properly known as the forestaysail, is often contracted to foresail.

Fore-and-aft rigged A ship on which the preponderance of sails are set with their leading edges attached to the masts is said to be fore-and-aft rigged. *cf.* Square-rigged

Gaff The spar from which the upper edge of a fore-and-aft sail is suspended.

Gun deck The deck, or decks, running the length of the ship on which the main armament was housed.

Half deck The longest of the tiers of part decks aft in a large ship. *cf.* Quarter deck and Poop deck

Heel over When a ship leans over in press of wind she is said to heel over.

Hogging A ship whose ends had drooped in relation to the middle of the hull was said to have hogged.

Jib The triangular sails set forward of the forestaysail (q.v.).

Keel The timber along the bottom of the hull forming the 'spine' of the ship.

Lateen A triangular sail set from a long yard. It originated in the Mediterranean (a corruption of 'Latin').

Lee-boards Boards let down on the leeward side of the hull of some flat-bottomed boats, to keep them from being blown sideways.

Leech The trailing edge, or aftermost edge, of a sail.

Leeward The side of a ship away from the wind (the opposite of windward).

Luff The leading, or front, edge of a sail.

Main deck The upper deck which ran the full length of the ship.

Marline spike A wooden or metal spike used to part the strands of a rope when splicing. Also used as an impromptu weapon.

Mess deck A lower deck on which the seamen's messes, or dining places, were situated.

Mizzen The smallest, aftermost mast of a ship.

Poop deck The smallest, aftermost deck of a large ship.

Quarters The after parts of the underwater hull of a ship.

Reef A sail is reefed when its area is reduced by temporarily gathering a section with ties or 'reef points'. Nowadays sails are often reduced by rolling the sail up on the boom (q.v.).

Rose The division of a circle into equal segments labelled either by names of winds or points of the compass.

Scandalize The reduction of the sail area by lowering the peak and hauling up the lower windward corner.

Sheer The curve of the top edge of a ship's bulwarks.

Ship-rigged A ship with three or more masts with square sails on all the masts except the lowest sail on the mizzen, which is always either a lateen sail or a gaff sail.

Shrouds The ropes forming the lateral supports of a mast. They often had light ropes fixed horizontally across them (ratlines) to assist sailors climbing the rigging.

Sinnet A multi-strand plait of light (thin) line. Sinnits, or sennets, may be flat, round, square, or polygonal. Used as straps, slings, and decoration.

Spar A generic term for the poles used as yards, booms, gaffs, etc. Occasionally, but not usually, also applied to the masts.

Spring A spar is said to be sprung when it is cracked or weakened. A spring is also a rope leading diagonally aft (or forward) from the bow (or stern) when a ship is moored alongside a quay.

Sprit The spar running diagonally up from the foot of the mast on which barges and wherries set their mainsails. *cf.* Bowsprit

Spritsail Spritsail has two meanings: the square sail set under the bowsprit (the Roman artemon) and the fore-and-aft sail set by barges and wherries.

Square-rigged A ship on which the preponderance of sails are set suspended from horizontal yards is said to be square-rigged. *cf.* Fore-and-aft rigged and Ship-rigged

Stays The ropes forming the fore-and-aft supports of a mast.

Swim-bowed Boats, usually barges or lighters, with no stem but a flat transom (q.v.) leaning forwards were said to be swim-bowed.

Tacking The zig-zag course that a sailing ship has to take in order to go to windward. The act of passing the ship's head through the eye of the wind.

Taffrail The 'balustrade' across the back of the uppermost, aftermost deck of a ship.

Top-gallant The sails set above the topsails.

Topmast The separate mast attached to, and reaching above, the lower mast upon which the topsails were set.

Topsail The sails set above the courses (q.v.).

Topsides The sides of the hull above the waterline.

Transom The flat stern of a ship above the waterline.

Truck The hardwood cap set on top of the uppermost mast to prevent rain penetrating and rotting it.

Trysail A small triangular sail set in place of a fore-and-aft sail, made of very heavy material for storm conditions.

Tumble-home If a ship is wider at the waterline than at the bulwarks (q.v.) her sides are said to tumble home.

Weatherly A ship which is capable of sailing close to the wind is called weatherly.

Well Measuring the depth of water inside a ship was known as 'sounding the well'.

Wind rose *See* Rose

Yard The spar from which a square, lateen, or lug sail is suspended.

Parts of a
of the seventeenth century
sailing ship

1. fore topsail
2. main topsail
3. foresail (fore course)
4. forecastle (fo'csle)
5. waist (amidships)
6. mainsail (main course)
7. mizzen sail
8. spritsail topsail
9. spritsail
10. forestay
11. topmast stay
12. bowsprit
13. spritsail topmast
14. shrouds
15. poop
16. taffrail
17. gallery
18. cat-head
19. ports
20. beak-head
21. fore top-gallant sail
22. main top-gallant sail

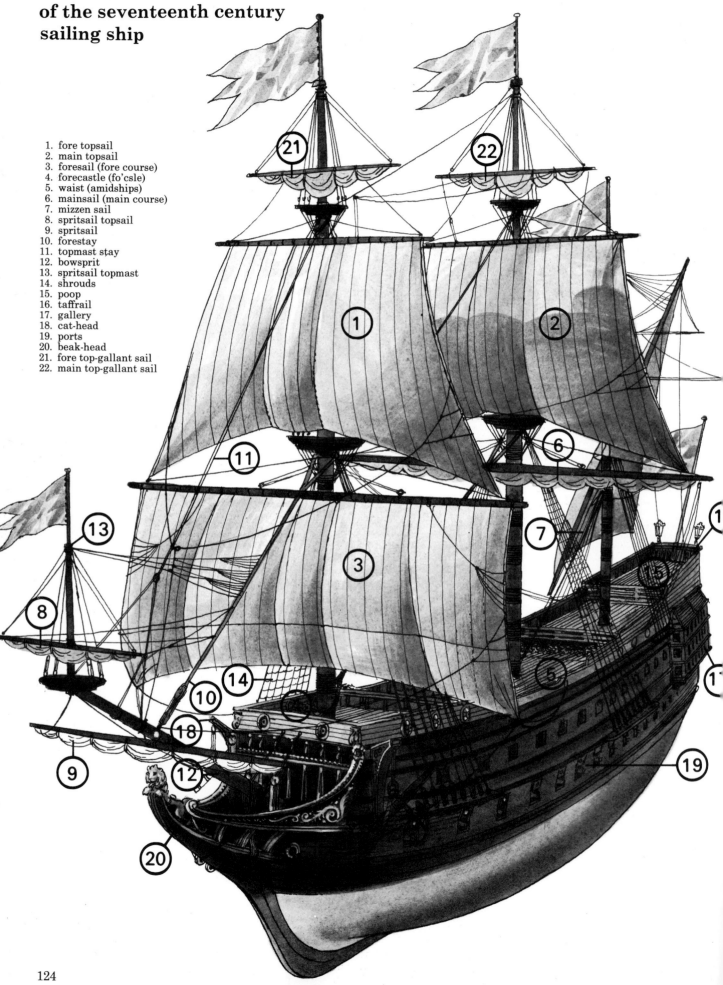

A short bibliography

Architectura Navalis Mercatoria (with *Tractat om Skepps-Byggeriet*) by Fredrik Henrik af Chapman. Reprint by Adlard Coles, London, 1971. Praeger, New York, 1971.

The Blackwall Frigates by Basil Lubbock, one of the Clipper Series. Brown, Glasgow, 1924.

The China Clippers by Basil Lubbock, one of the Clipper Series. Brown, Glasgow, 1950.

A Handbook of Sailing Barges by F.S. Cooper and J. Chancellor. Adlard Coles, Southampton, 1955.

The Haven-Finding Art by Eva G.R. Taylor. Hollis & Carter, London, 1956. Abelard-Schuman, New York, 1957.

The History of American Sailing Ships by Howard I. Chapelle. W.W. Norton, New York, 1935. Putnam, London, 1937.

The History of the American Sailing Navy by Howard I. Chapelle. W.W. Norton, New York, 1949. Allen and Unwin, London, 1950.

Journals on His Voyages of Discovery by Captain James Cook, edited by John C. Beaglehole. Cambridge University Press for the Hakluyt Society, 1955-67.

The Mathematical Practitioners of Hanoverian England by Eva G.R. Taylor. Cambridge University Press, 1966.

The Mathematical Practitioners of Tudor and Stuart England by Eva G.R. Taylor. Cambridge University Press, 1954.

Merchant Ships: a pictorial study by John H. La Dage and others. Cornell Maritime Press, Cambridge, Maryland, 1955. Putnam, London, 1955.

The Rigging of Ships in the Days of the Spritsail Topmast 1600-1720 by Roger C. Anderson. Publications of the Marine Research Society, volume 14, Salem, 1927.

Sailing Barges by Frank G.G. Carr. Peter Davies, London, 1951.

The Sailing Ship: six thousand years of history by Romola and Roger C. Anderson. Harrap, London, 1926.

Sailing Ships (volumes 1-11) by Geoffrey S. Laird Clowes. Science Museum, London, 1932-52.

The Search for Speed under Sail: 1700-1855 by Howard I. Chapelle. W.W. Norton, New York, 1967. Allen and Unwin, London, 1968.

Seventeenth-century Rigging: a handbook for model makers by Roger C. Anderson. Percival Marshall, London, 1955, and New York, 1957.

The Ship: an illustrated history by Björn Landstrom. Doubleday, New York, 1961. Allen and Unwin, London, 1961.

Index

Acknowledgments

The Wooden Midshipman on page 31 is reproduced by courtesy of the Trustees of the Dickens House and the drawing on page 117 by courtesy of the Syndics of the University Library, Cambridge.

Photographs
Alinari, Florence 11; H.R. Allen, Westerham 90 top, 90 bottom, 91 top, 91 bottom; Archives Photographiques, Paris 10 bottom; Barnabys Picture Library, London 115; British Museum, London 29 right; Central Press Photos Ltd, London 93; City Museum & Art Gallery, Hong Kong 46 top; Conway Picture Library, London 100-101; Crown Copyright. Science Museum, London 16 top, 28-29, 34, 35, 40 left, 40 right, 112-113; F.E. Gibson, St. Mary's, Isles of Scilly 120, 121, 122; Ambrose Greenway–Paul Popper Ltd 1, 2-3, 4-5; Hamlyn Group– Hawkley Studio Associates 21 top, 21 bottom, 33, 52, 62-63, 84 bottom, 86, 87, 103, 107 top, 108; Hamlyn Group Picture Library 13, 18 bottom, 31 left, 31 top right, 31 bottom right, 104 top left, 104-105 top, 104-105 bottom, 105 top right, 105 bottom right, 110-111; Hirmer Verlag, Munich 10 top; Hudson's Bay Company, London 43 top; Irish Tourist Board, Dublin 15; Keystone Press Agency Ltd, London 106; L.E.A., London 74; Lowndes Lodge Gallery, London SW1. 114; Mansell Collection, London 24 left, 24-25; Bildarchiv Foto Marburg 9; Mariners Museum, Newport News, Virginia 68 top, 68 bottom, 75 bottom; Maryland Historical Society, Baltimore, Maryland 67 top; Museum Plantin-Moretus en Prentenkabinet, Antwerp 42-43, 44; Nationaal Scheepvaartmuseum, Antwerp 22-23; National Library of Australia, Canberra 54; National Maritime Museum, Greenwich 26-27, 30, 32, 37, 39, 41, 45 bottom, 48, 49, 50-51, 55 top, 55 bottom, 58-59, 60, 61, 64-65, 69, 70, 75 top, 78-79, 81 top, 89 bottom, 92-93, 109, 113 top, 118, 119 top, 119 bottom; Nederlandsch Historisch Scheepvaart Museum, Amsterdam 36, 38, 47, 56-57; New York Public Library, New York 67; Notman Photographic Archives, McCord Museum of McGill University, Montreal 96 left; P.A.–Reuter, London 95 top; P & O Shipping Company, London 92 top; Peabody Museum, Salem, Massachusetts 6-7, 73 top right, 73 bottom right, 82-83; Pictor Ltd, London 19; Picturepoint Ltd, London 94, 95 bottom, 98, 107 bottom; Radio Times Hulton Picture Library, London 46 bottom; San Francisco Maritime Museum, San Francisco, California endpapers, 72-73, 96-97, 101 top, 101 bottom; K. Scholz–Bavaria 18 top; K. Scholz–Z.E.F.A. 99; Science Museum, London 12, 45 top, 53, 80-81, 84-85 top, 88 top, 88 bottom, 89 top; Staatsarchiv, Hamburg 17 top, 27 top; Staten Island Historical Society, Richmondtown, Staten Island, New York 76; Universitetets Oldsaksamling, Oslo 16-17; University Library, Cambridge 117; Whaling Museum, New Bedford, Massachusetts 71.